No-First-Use

sipri

Stockholm International Peace Research Institute

SIPRI is an independent institute for research into problems
of peace and conflict, especially those of arms control and
disarmament. It was established in 1966 to commemorate
Sweden's 150 years of unbroken peace.

The institute is financed by the Swedish Parliament. The staff,
the Governing Board and the Scientific Council are
international.

Governing Board

Rolf Björnerstedt, Chairman (Sweden)
Egon Bahr (FR Germany)
Francesco Calogero (Italy)
Tim Greve (Norway)
Max Jakobson (Finland)
Karlheinz Lohs
   (German Democratic Republic)
Emma Rothschild (United Kingdom)
The Director

Director

Frank Blackaby (United Kingdom)

sipri

Stockholm International Peace Research Institute
Bergshamra, S-171 73 Solna, Sweden
Cable: Peaceresearch, Stockholm
Telephone: 08-55 97 00

No-First-Use

Edited by
Frank Blackaby
Jozef Goldblat
Sverre Lodgaard

sipri

Stockholm International Peace Research Institute

Taylor & Francis
London and Philadelphia
1984

| UK | Taylor & Francis Ltd, 4 John St, London WC1N 2ET |
| USA | Taylor & Francis Inc., 242 Cherry St, Philadelphia, PA 19106–1906 |

British Library Cataloguing in Publication Data

No-first-use
  1. Atomic warfare
  I. Blackaby, F. T. II. Goldblat, Jozef
  III. Lodgaard, Sverre
  355'.0217   U263

  ISBN 0-85066-274-5
  ISBN 0-85066-260-5 Pbk

Library of Congress Cataloging in Publication Data

Main entry under title:

No-first-use

  Includes bibliographical references and index.
  1. No first use (Nuclear strategy) I. Blackaby, Frank Thomas.
II. Goldblat, Jozef. III. Lodgaard, Sverre. IV. Stockholm
International Peace Research Institute.
U264.N6 1984   327.1'74   84-2467
ISBN 0-85066-274-5
ISBN 0-85066-260-5 Pbk

*Typesetting by Georgia Origination, Liverpool L3 9EG
Printed in Great Britain by Taylor & Francis (Printers) Ltd,
Basingstoke, Hants.*

Preface

The proposal to renounce the first use of nuclear weapons has become a focal point of the current debate concerning the deployment of nuclear weapons in Europe. The purpose of this book, which is intended as a contribution to the debate, is twofold: *first*, to take stock of the arguments which have been put forward by the proponents and the opponents of no-first-use; and *second*, to examine the political, military and arms control implications of such a commitment.

Part I provides an introduction, a summary of the main points made in the various papers, and, finally, the conclusions of the three authors.

In part II of this book, two seminal articles are reproduced which served to bring the issue to the forefront of discussion. SIPRI then invited nine eminent people to comment on the questions raised by these articles: their papers comprise part III.

It is hoped that the present book will be of use not only to politicians, diplomats and scholars, but also to other concerned citizens.

Frank Blackaby
Jozef Goldblat
Sverre Lodgaard

Stockholm, April 1984

Contents

PART II. NO-FIRST-USE—MAIN ARGUMENTS FOR AND AGAINST

PART III. DISCUSSION PAPERS

Part I
No-first-use of nuclear weapons— an overview

No-first-use of nuclear weapons—an overview

Frank Blackaby, Jozef Goldblat and Sverre Lodgaard

This chapter is in three sections. The introduction explains why the no-first-use issue is now topical—the pressures that have arisen from discussion in the churches, among international lawyers, at the United Nations, and among military thinkers. The second section summarizes the arguments presented in Parts II and III of the book. The third section contains the conclusions of the three authors of this chapter.

I. Introduction

Should any nation ever consider that it has the right to be the first to use nuclear weapons? More specifically, should NATO change its existing strategy of 'flexible response', which allows for the possibility of responding to a conventional attack with nuclear weapons?

The debate on these issues in recent years has been conducted on a number of fronts. A first use of nuclear weapons has come under challenge from many different directions: from church synods, from international lawyers, in debates in the United Nations, and from strategic thinkers.

The churches and the moral issue

The Archbishop of Canterbury recently said that "Christians can never have an easy conscience about nuclear weapons".[1] That unease has been growing, in parallel with the greater concern among the general public. In most of the recent church assemblies and synods, the issue of nuclear weapons has been on the agenda: it has often been the most prominent item.

Some of the resolutions have been of too general a nature to have much impact on policy—for example a resolution endorsing the view that "nuclear arms . . . are by their nature morally wrong".[2] Other resolutions express what might appropriately be called pious hopes—one, for example, urging "controlled verifiable measures of multilateral disarmament leading to the total elimination of all nuclear weapons within five years".[3] However, many of the churches—like many of the peace movements—have now put considerable effort into the study of problems raised by nuclear weapons. They can no longer be written off as ignorant innocents. The pastoral letter of the US National Conference of Catholic Bishops in particular shows evidence of wide reading in the relevant military literature.[4] This is probably the most important document among the many that have come from church sources on nuclear weapons, for two reasons: first, because the United States is one of the two major nuclear powers; and second, because the Catholic Church can claim over 50 million adherents in the United States.

The pastoral letter—which was approved by a large majority in May 1983—gave a highly conditional acceptance of the doctrine of deterrence. It quoted Pope John Paul II's message to the UN Special Session on Disarmament:

In current conditions 'deterrence' based on balance, certainly not as an end in itself but as a step on the way toward a progressive disarmament, may still be judged morally acceptable. Nonetheless, in order to ensure peace, it is indispensable not to be satisfied with this minimum which is always susceptible to the real danger of explosion. (Pope John Paul II, "Message to U.N. Special Session on Disarmament".)[5]

It added:

Deterrence is not an adequate strategy as a long-term basis for peace; it is a transitional strategy justifiable only in conjunction with resolute determination to pursue arms control and disarmament. We are convinced that the 'fundamental principle on which our present peace depends must be replaced by another, which declares that the true and solid peace of nations consists not in equality of arms but in mutual trust alone.' (Pope John XXIII, *Peace on Earth*)[5]

However, together with this conditional acceptance of deterrence, there was a categorical rejection of the first use of nuclear weapons. To quote from the summary:

The Initiation of Nuclear War: We do not perceive any situation in which the deliberate initiation of nuclear war, on however restricted a scale, can be morally justified. Non-nuclear attacks by another state must be resisted by other than nuclear means. Therefore, a serious moral obligation exists to develop non-nuclear defensive strategies as rapidly as possible. In this letter we urge NATO to move rapidly toward the adoption of a "no first use" policy, but we recognize this will take time to implement and will require the development of an adequate alternative defense posture.[6]

This position—that the first use of nuclear weapons is morally unacceptable—seems common to most church resolutions on the subject of nuclear weapons.

In Britain, the leader of the Catholic Church (Cardinal Basil Hume, Archbishop of Westminster) has endorsed the highly conditional acceptance of deterrence in the Pope's statement to the UN Second Special Session. The Cardinal's statement, however, does not explicitly address the question of first use—though there is a strong implication that it would not be morally acceptable.[7] (There are some countries in which the churches have avoided the nuclear weapon issue: in France, for example, the idea of a conference of French Catholic bishops pronouncing on the morality of nuclear weapons has been dismissed as "inconceivable".[8]) Some church resolutions condemn all use of nuclear weapons and so do not have to address themselves specifically to the no-first-use issue. Those which do treat this issue separately tend to take the same position as the US Catholic bishops. For example, the synod of the Scottish Episcopal [Anglican] Church called for moves towards a no-first-use policy regarding nuclear weapons.[9] The same position was taken by the Council of the Evangelical Church in FR Germany.[10] The General Synod of the Church of England, in February 1983, rejected a motion calling for unilateral nuclear disarmament—and this was the feature of that debate which attracted most attention. However, the Synod did reject first use. It adopted a resolution which reads as follows:

That the Synod . . .
(i) affirms that it is the duty of Her Majesty's Government and her allies to maintain adequate forces to guard against nuclear blackmail and to deter nuclear and non-nuclear aggressors;
(ii) asserts that the tactics and strategies of this country and her NATO allies should be seen to be unmistakeably defensive in respect of the countries of the Warsaw Pact;
(iii) judges that even a small-scale first use of nuclear weapons could never be morally justified in view of the high risk that this would lead to full-scale nuclear warfare;
(iv) believes that there is a moral obligation on all countries (including the members of NATO) publicly to forswear the first use of nuclear weapons in any form;
(v) bearing in mind that many in Europe live in fear of nuclear catastrophe and that nuclear parity is not essential to deterrence, calls on Her Majesty's Government to take immediate steps in conjunction with her allies to further the principles embodied in this motion so as to reduce progressively NATO's dependence on nuclear weapons and to decrease nuclear arsenals throughout the world.[11]

The authorities—and to some extent, military commanders—have begun to realize that these expressions of concern in church assemblies are matters of some importance. This, again, has been particularly true in the USA, which (by comparison with most European countries) is a church-going country. (In Britain the government seems to have taken little notice of the Anglican synod's resolution.) In the USA, there have been some rather anguished articles in military or strategic journals.[12] In one, it was suggested that the position taken by the US Catholic bishops differed substantially from that of the Pope himself;[13] the evidence for this seems weak.[14] A number of members of the US Administration had tried in various ways to influence the drafters of the Catholic pastoral letter—sometimes in a rather ham-fisted way: a letter to the Bishops' Commission from National Security Advisor William Clark was released to the press before it reached the bishops. The bishops appear to have been "more irritated by the tactics than impressed with the arguments".[15] Whereas the bishops went to considerable pains to understand the military and strategic issues, their critics in the US Administration do not seem to have made any comparable efforts to understand Christian ethics. In particular, they have failed to grasp that Christian ethics is not just a sub-branch of utilitarianism. Christian morality is not a simple morality of consequences, in which the morality of an action is

5

judged simply from a summing up of its consequences in comparison with those of alternative courses of action.[16] Given the extreme difficulty of predicting the total consequences of many actions, the tradition of Christian ethics accepts the idea that certain courses of action should be unconditionally rejected.

To sum up: most church assemblies or synods which have considered the matter have judged the first use of nuclear weapons to be morally unacceptable. Bishops may carry less weight in this matter than generals, but in the long run church opinion is a force of some significance.

International law and no-first-use

Although there is no treaty specifically outlawing nuclear weapons, a number of international lawyers question the legality of the use of these weapons. One can envisage the following situations in which nuclear weapons might well be resorted to: (a) in a surprise pre-emptive attack aimed at disarming the adversary by eliminating his strategic nuclear potential; (b) in the course of escalating hostilities started with conventional weapons; and (c) as a reprisal for nuclear attack.

The first situation, usually referred to as 'first strike', is covered by the fundamental rule of international law, enshrined in the UN Charter, which prohibits aggression, irrespective of the type of weapon used.

The third situation normally applies to an act performed in response to a preceding illegality. Such an act, even if illegal *per se*, is usually considered to be in order, as long as it is proportionate in scale.

It is the second situation which is usually referred to as 'first use', and which applies to the employment of nuclear weapons in war in retaliation for the use of conventional weapons, that is the most controversial, because it involves the right to self-defence. The question is whether, and to what extent, this right is limited under international law.

The point of departure for the examination of the legal status of nuclear weapons is the rule embodied in the 1907 Hague Convention on land warfare that the right of belligerents to injure the enemy is not unlimited. It is prohibited to employ arms which cause "unnecessary" suffering, or to destroy the enemy's property, unless such destruction is "imperatively demanded" by the necessities of war. Since nuclear explosions could produce uncontrollable biological and environmental consequences and cause massive injury to people and massive damage to property, and since mass destruction can hardly be a necessity, the observance of the above rule of warfare may be difficult, if not impossible. For there is absolutely no guarantee that nuclear warfare can be kept limited in scale once the nuclear threshold has been crossed.

Moreover, under customary international law, which makes a clear distinction between combatants and non-combatants, and between military and non-military targets, and which was reiterated in the 1949 Geneva Conventions for the protection of war victims, the belligerents are under strict obligation to protect the civilians, who take no part in hostilities, against the consequences of war. The indiscriminate nature of nuclear weapons renders this rule impossible to comply with, too. Even if only military targets were aimed at, civilian casualties would be an inevitable by-product, and in many cases might outnumber the military ones by far.

Yet another iniquitous aspect of nuclear warfare is the inability of the belligerents to comply with the important demand of the world order to respect the inviolability of the territory of neutral powers. For it is impossible to confine the effects of nuclear explosions, particularly radioactive contamination, to the territories of the states at war.

Non-nuclear weapon states which have nuclear weapons deployed on their territories would not even be in a position to declare themselves neutral in a war between the nuclear weapon powers.

Furthermore, nuclear radiation and radioactive fall-out always inflict damage on the biological tissue of humans, animals and plants. It can, therefore, from the point of view of international law, be compared to poison, the use of which is already prohibited as a method of warfare. Indeed, the 1925 Geneva Protocol bans the use in war of asphyxiating, poisonous or other gases, and of all analogous liquids, materials or devices, in addition to bacteriological methods of warfare.

And finally, it is worth noting that, in placing restraints on the conduct of hostilities, the Hague Conventions included a rule, known as the Martens Clause, which makes usages established "among civilized peoples", the laws of humanity, and the dictates of public conscience obligatory by themselves even in the absence of a specific treaty prohibiting a particular type of weapon. It was this legal yardstick that the International Military Tribunal, convened at Nuremberg to prosecute Nazi leaders after World War II, applied in concluding that the law of war is to be found not only in treaties, but in customs and practices of states, which gradually obtained universal recognition, as well as in judicial decisions.

The cumulative effect of those restrictions is such that nuclear war cannot be initiated with obedience to the rules of international law.

East–West policies

The first international controversy regarding nuclear weapons arose as early as 1946, when the Soviet Union proposed that the production and use of these weapons should be prohibited, and that they should be destroyed within a very short period of time. This was a reaction to the US (so-called Baruch) plan, which provided for an international system of control of atomic energy, including sanctions for infringements; nuclear disarmament was to be considered only after such a system had been firmly established. But the USSR was at that time considerably less advanced in the atomic field than the USA and would not accept any scheme that could have led to preservation of the US monopoly of nuclear weapons.

Even later, after it had itself acquired nuclear weapons, the USSR continued to insist on a prohibition on use as a first step towards a comprehensive programme of disarmament. On the other hand, taking advantage of its nuclear preponderance, which was overwhelming in the 1950s, the USA pursued a policy which implied the possibility of massive use of nuclear weapons against the Soviet Union in response even to low levels of aggression carried out with conventional forces.

Subsequently, in the 1960s, as a consequence of the growing Soviet nuclear capability, the USA and NATO adopted a strategy of 'flexible response', which still constitutes the essence of the Western deterrence policy. That strategy calls for the Alliance to initiate nuclear war with battlefield nuclear weapons if conventional defences fail, and to escalate the type of nuclear weapon used, as necessary, up to and including the use of strategic forces against targets in the Soviet Union. The official US position is that since there is no rule of international law expressly prohibiting states from the use of nuclear weapons in warfare, the use of such weapons against enemy combatants and other military objectives is permitted. The 1977 Protocol I (additional to the 1949 Geneva Conventions) relating to the protection of victims of international armed conflicts prohibits methods or means of warfare which are intended to cause widespread, long-term and severe damage to the natural environment, and also those that may be expected to do so.[17] However, in signing the Protocol, the USA stated its understanding that the rules established therein were not intended to have any effect on and do not regulate or prohibit the use of nuclear weapons.

Only once, in 1955, did the East–West positions seem to coincide. The Soviet Union then accepted the Anglo-French proposal for the prohibition of the use of nuclear weapons to become effective after 75 per cent of agreed reductions of armed forces and conventional armaments had been carried out. Nevertheless, this compromise, which reflected a recognition of the intimate link between nuclear and conventional armaments, was not endorsed by the USA. At the 1955 Geneva summit meeting, the Soviet Union submitted a proposal for the reduction of armaments and the prohibition of nuclear weapons, and suggested that, pending the conclusion of a convention on such reduction and prohibition, the heads of government of France, the USSR, the United Kingdom and the United States assume the obligation not to be the first to use nuclear weapons against any country. This was the first time that the Soviet Union made a no-first-use proposal.

A few years later, the USA proposed that the parties should agree not to use nuclear weapons unless they were subjected to conventional attack that (in the judgement of the side attacked) could not be stopped by conventional forces. The Soviet Union rejected the proposed formula as "legitimizing" nuclear weapons.

The United Nations

The very first resolution of the UN General Assembly, adopted unanimously in 1946, set as a goal the "control of atomic energy to the extent necessary to ensure its use only for peaceful purposes".[18] In subsequent years, several specific proposals regarding the use of nuclear weapons have been discussed. The most important action in this regard was taken in 1961, when the General Assembly, by a vote of 55 to 20, with 26 abstentions, adopted a declaration stating that the use of nuclear weapons was contrary to the spirit, letter and aims of the United Nations and, as such, a direct violation of the UN Charter. The resolution went on to proclaim such use to be a "crime against mankind and civilization".[19] The USA and other NATO countries opposed the resolution, while the USSR and its allies supported it. The US position, then spelled out, was that in the event of an aggression that could not be repulsed by conventional forces, the USA must be prepared to take whatever action with whatever weapons were appropriate.

In addition to its pronouncement on the illegality of nuclear weapons, the UN General Assembly asked the Secretary-General to ascertain the views of the governments of member states on the possibility of convening a special conference for signing a convention on the "prohibition of the use of nuclear and thermo-nuclear weapons for war purposes".[19] However, the Secretary-General's consultations with governments proved inconclusive and, in spite of repeated appeals by the Assembly, the requested conference was never convened.

Another important resolution, which was adopted at the initiative of the Soviet Union in 1972 by 73 votes to 4, with 46 abstentions (including the Western nuclear powers), contained a declaration on the renunciation of the use or threat of force in international relations and the permanent prohibition of the use of nuclear weapons.[20] However, in establishing a strict linkage between the postulated non-use of nuclear weapons and the principle of non-use of force, the proclaimed prohibition, in fact, licensed the first use of nuclear weapons in defence against an aggression committed with conventional means of warfare. This is all the more so, since it emphasized the "inalienable" right to self-defence, implying that states may make use of any means they deem appropriate in the exercise of this right.

Resolutions calling for a ban on the use of nuclear weapons have also been considered later, mainly at the initiative of India and the Soviet Union. Of those passed in 1983, one resolution, adopted by 126 votes to 17, with 6 abstentions, requested the Committee on Disarmament to commence negotiations in order to achieve agreement on an international convention prohibiting the use or threat of use of nuclear weapons "under any circumstances",[21] while the other resolution, passed by 95 votes to 19, with 30 abstentions, "resolutely, unconditionally and for all time" condemned nuclear war, as well as political and military doctrines and concepts intended to provide "legitimacy" for the first use of nuclear weapons and in general to justify the "admissibility" of unleashing nuclear war.[22] These resolutions were also opposed by the Western nuclear powers and have remained dead letters.

Unilateral commitments

In 1982, the Soviet Union formally pledged itself not to be the first to use nuclear weapons, but it added a caveat that in the formulation of its policy it would take into account whether other powers followed its example. This pledge complemented the declaration made by the USSR four years before that it would never use nuclear weapons against states which had renounced the production and acquisition of such weapons and did not have them on their territories. China is committed, since 1964, not to be the first to use nuclear weapons at any time and under any circumstances.

Other nuclear weapon powers maintain that they cannot assume such a sweeping obligation as long as there is a threat of war. They have undertaken to renounce the first use of nuclear weapons only under certain conditions. Thus, the USA announced that it would not use nuclear weapons against any non-nuclear weapon state which is party to the Non-Proliferation Treaty or any comparable internationally binding agreement not to acquire nuclear explosive devices, except in the case of an attack on the USA or its allies by a non-nuclear weapon state allied to or associated with a nuclear weapon state in carrying out or sustaining the attack. A similar statement was issued by the UK. France said that it would not use nuclear arms against a state that does not have these weapons and has pledged not to seek them. However, France too made it clear that its no-use guarantee would not apply in the case of an act of aggression carried out in association or in alliance with a nuclear weapon state against France or against a state with which France has a security commitment. (See appendix I.)

The qualifications referred to above were phrased in such a way as to suit the current nuclear doctrines of the great powers. Analogous language was used in the interpretative declarations to Additional Protocol II of the 1967 Treaty of Tlatelolco, the only international agreement relating to non-use, which all the nuclear weapon states have signed and ratified, and which provides for an undertaking to respect the statute of military denuclearization of Latin America. It should be noted, however, that these declarations amount to reservations, which are not permitted by the provisions of the Treaty applicable to the Protocol.

In the past few years efforts have been made in the Geneva-based Committee on Disarmament to develop 'negative' security assurances, that is, assurances of no use of nuclear weapons against non-nuclear weapon states, which would be uniform and free of limitations, conditions or exceptions. These efforts have so far yielded no result, mainly because of differing perceptions of security interests. But even if some compromise formula were found, the very assurances which are being sought would be of questionable value. The consequences of a nuclear war on a global or regional scale would not spare states enjoying a 'no-use guarantee'. Moreover, all nuclear weapon powers possess conventional armed forces superior to those of their potential non-nuclear adversaries and would not need to have recourse to nuclear weapons to stop an aggression committed by the latter. Still, providing unconditional assurances of no use of nuclear weapons against non-nuclear weapon states would require major changes in the postures and policies of the great powers, especially the USA. Such changes would facilitate the adoption of a universal policy of no-first-use.

Other challenges

None of the groups or institutions so far considered—the churches, international law, the United Nations or disarmament negotiating bodies—has proved powerful enough to have much impact as yet on strategic policy. The most influential challenge in the West to the first use of nuclear weapons has come not from these groups, but from individuals who have previously been prominent in the defence or arms control establishments. The seminal article in this regard is the one by McGeorge Bundy, George F. Kennan, Robert S. McNamara and Gerard Smith, published in *Foreign Affairs* in Spring 1982, and reproduced in this book on pages 29–41. All four authors had played a prominent part in the formation of US security and arms control policies during the preceding two decades.

In sum, the challenges to a doctrine which permits the first use of nuclear weapons are challenges on a number of fronts. Further, the challenges are coming from well-established institutions, and from individuals who cannot be regarded as fringe radicals. The doctrine of the first use of nuclear weapons is therefore a good candidate for re-examination.

II. Summary of the main arguments

The purpose of this section is to summarize the arguments used in the various papers in this book on the issues raised by a no-first-use declaration. The papers present a wide range of assessments—from enthusiastic endorsement of the idea at one extreme to outright condemnation at the other.

The question at issue is not simply whether other nations possessing nuclear weapons should follow China and the Soviet Union in making a no-first-use declaration. There is another question which is perhaps more important: what changes in the characteristics of nuclear weapons as well as in the structure and deployment of both nuclear and conventional forces should logically follow if the United States, as well as the Soviet Union, were to agree to renounce the first use of nuclear weapons?

Declaratory policy

One common argument is that a pledge of no-first-use is simply a piece of declaratory policy—it cannot constitute a guarantee. A pledge of this kind, it is suggested, would leave things exactly as they are. Neither side would trust the other and so neither side would make any change in its weaponry or deployment. Of course, if each side assumed that the other side was not serious, and if neither side made any changes in its military posture, then indeed such a pledge would be empty. If that were the case, then it could not of course at the same time be argued that such a pledge would be damaging to security.

However, it is sometimes suggested on the NATO side that there would be an asymmetry. If NATO made a no-first-use declaration, it would be forced by public opinion to make consequential changes in its deployment of nuclear weapons. The Warsaw Treaty Organization (WTO) would be under no such pressure. This, it is argued, would be damaging to NATO's security. The implication is clear: the changes in nuclear deployment which would logically follow from a no-first-use declaration would have to be mutually agreed.

The proposition that a pledge of no-first-use would be empty implies that declarations about the conduct of war are of no importance, since such undertakings can never be dependable once war has begun. This is a sweeping conclusion: one comment suggests that it is tantamount to burying the laws of war. However, in spite of their inherent weaknesses these laws, setting limits on permissible violence, have been useful. Thus the 1925 Geneva Protocol concerning chemical and bacteriological weapons is an outstanding example of a widely accepted no-first-use commitment which continues to deter recourse to these weapons.

Another line of attack on no-first-use commitments has been to say that the outlawing of the first use of nuclear weapons might appear to justify the first use of conventional weapons. Again, this is a criticism which does not seem to have been levelled at other rules related to the conduct of war. Once again the Geneva Protocol is relevant. Because most states have agreed not to be the first to use chemical weapons, it cannot be argued that this makes it legal for them to be the first to use other weapons.

However, it does seem fair to say that declarations of no-first-use of nuclear weapons should logically lead to changes in the composition, characteristics and deployment of nuclear forces. "So long as both sides deploy thousands of tactical nuclear weapons in close proximity to the borders that divide the NATO countries from those of the WTO, statements by the leaders of either side that they will not be the first to utilize them are of little practical value" (see Warnke, page 122). If war broke out in Europe and one side or the other found that its stocks of tactical nuclear weapons were in danger of being overrun, the temptation to use them rather than lose them would be very strong. A no-first-use declaration ought to lead to the withdrawal of nuclear weapons which have war-fighting rather than deterrent functions; and it is certainly incompatible with such a declaration to introduce short-range nuclear weapons into forward areas.

The case for no-first-use

The basic argument for NATO's adoption of a policy of no-first-use of nuclear weapons is this. If ever NATO were to make a nuclear response to a conventional attack, it would be a suicidal act. The Soviet Union would surely retaliate with its own nuclear weapons. Further, "no one has ever succeeded in advancing any persuasive reason to believe that any use of nuclear weapons, even on the smallest scale, could reliably be expected to remain limited" (see Bundy *et al.*, page 32). So NATO's first use of nuclear weapons would in all probability lead to the destruction of the territory which NATO was established to defend.

Of course the proposition is put forward that the threat to use nuclear weapons is made in order to avoid ever having to execute it—sometimes with the implication that although the first use of nuclear weapons might be threatened, in the event no attempt would be made to make good that threat. However, the efficacy of a threat depends on its credibility. To make the threat credible, the use of nuclear weapons must be explicitly incorporated into military planning. That means, in turn, that the military might well find that they had no alternative to the first use of nuclear weapons, since their planning had been based on that assumption.

The negative case against a strategy which involves the first use of nuclear weapons is, then, that it is potentially suicidal. However, the proponents of a no-first-use commitment point to possible positive consequences as well.

Once the nuclear powers had all made such a commitment it should lead to the agreed elimination of those nuclear weapons which are not explicitly for the purpose of deterrence. An even stronger claim is made by some other proponents. In the words of Chairman Brezhnev's message to the UN Second Special Session on Disarmament, "If the other nuclear Powers assume an equally precise and clear obligation not to be the first to use nuclear weapons, that would be tantamount in practice to a ban on the use of nuclear weapons altogether, which is espoused by the overwhelming majority of the countries of the world".[23]

The case against no-first-use

The case against such a commitment by NATO is as follows. The Soviet Union has a massive superiority in conventional weaponry in Europe. It is deterred from using it because of the risk that if it did, it might set off a nuclear war. If that risk were removed, NATO's defence would cease to be unpredictable, and would become "predictably inadequate."

The Soviet Commander in Chief... would know in advance that he was free to concentrate his forces, rather than having to disperse them to minimize the threat from US nuclear weapons. He would be virtually invited to make full use of his superior numbers so as to bring a superior weight of fire to bear at a point or points of his choosing... the effectiveness of conventional forces is directly proportional to their degree of concentration and to the weight of metal they can launch on a target. (See Gallois, page 95.)

So the effect of a no-first-use declaration by the United States would be to make a war in Europe more likely. It is because of that conventional superiority, it is argued, that the Soviet Union advocates no-first-use of nuclear weapons; it is aware that under such a regime it would have overwhelming military superiority. Certain critics of a NATO no-first-use commitment go further. It would, they say, damage European confidence in US security guarantees and would probably be followed at some stage by a US withdrawal from Europe. NATO would fall to pieces and the Soviet Union could impose its will on the countries of western Europe.

Strengthening NATO's conventional forces

Those who argue for a NATO no-first-use commitment usually (but not always) link it with the need to improve NATO's capacity to fight a conventional war—on the grounds that the WTO has conventional superiority in Europe.

A full assessment of the balance of conventional forces in Europe is not attempted in this book. Simple comparisons of stocks of particular kinds of weapon are, of course, inadequate. Comparisons must also include questions of alliance strength and morale—for example, the question of whether the military forces of Poland and the German Democratic Republic would willingly join in an offensive across the border between the two Germanies. The papers present a range of judgements on the conventional balance. There is the view that rough conventional parity exists (see Milshtein, page 119), so that no changes in NATO conventional deployment are needed. On the other hand, there is the view that the WTO has a margin of superiority which is so great that no plausible programme of conventional rearmament on the NATO side could do much to bridge the gap (see Gallois, page 93).

One problem, of course, is that although any country or alliance may try to improve its relative military position unilaterally, the potential enemy may not allow it to do so. If NATO were to decide to spend more on conventional weapons, then the WTO might well decide to do the same, leaving the relative position unchanged. This—it is suggested—would be quite likely if NATO's conventional rearmament simply consisted of strengthening its present deployment; for this would be seen by the other side as strengthening NATO's offensive capabilities. "All these armies in Europe are the children of Hitler's tank armies, designed for attack and *Blitzkrieg* in World War II" (see Afheldt, page 59). An alternative approach is suggested, to construct a pattern of non-nuclear defence for NATO which could not be regarded as offensive. The proposal, discussed by Afheldt, page 61, is that of a West German study group on alternative security policies. It suggests, *inter alia*, that the defence structure should be one which does not offer important targets for WTO nuclear weapons. The proposal is based on three pillars: a pioneer-infantry network of small units, dispersed all over the country; a network of precision-guided artillery rockets; and an information network. It follows the general principle of making only such military preparations as those which could be accepted on the enemy's side as preparations which do not increase the threat.

Another possible solution suggested is a negotiated reduction of conventional forces to levels which would make a successful attack impossible.

Other options

The choice of policy in this matter is not exclusively between pure and simple 'first-use' and 'no-first-use' postures; other options exist. A no-first-use posture can be made conditional—only to be adopted when certain other things have been done. Thus it can be—and often is—made conditional on the strengthening of

NATO's conventional capacity. Another possibility is that it should be made conditional on the adoption of confidence-building measures which substantially reduce the risk of conventional attack in Europe. An example of such a confidence-building measure is a 100-km wide corridor on either side of the dividing line in Europe, from which all nuclear armaments, as well as conventional armaments perceived as offensive, are withdrawn. Then there is the option of 'no-early-first-use': in other words, raising the nuclear threshold. The Supreme Allied Commander, Europe (SACEUR), General Bernard Rogers, has welcomed this idea. However, unless accompanied by the withdrawal of nuclear weapons from forward positions, it could be used as an excuse for simply adding more conventional weapons to the existing stock of nuclear warheads. This option would also forgo some of the potential benefits from a clear statement of no-first-use.

Deterrence and war-fighting

Those who advocate a no-first-use posture point out that nuclear weapons would still be there to act as a deterrent. The commitment would remain to respond with nuclear weapons to any first use of them by the other side. "It would still be necessary to be ready to reply with American nuclear weapons to any nuclear attack on the Federal Republic" (see Bundy *et al.*, page 33). The deterrent function of nuclear weapons would not be removed. Some question these conclusions. Under a no-first-use regime, the USA, it is suggested, would withdraw its nuclear weapons from Europe. This would be the first step in a process of disengagement. The US forces in western Europe would then appear unprotected, and there would be strong pressure for their withdrawal as well. Although the United States might declare that it would respond with nuclear weapons to any nuclear attack on FR Germany, this statement would be increasingly disbelieved.

The contrary view is that the situation would change by stationing on west European soil nuclear weapons that can strike the Soviet Union. However, the Soviet Union, if attacked by US nuclear weapons, is likely to reply with an attack on the United States anyway, regardless of whether the US warheads are launched from FR Germany or from the USA.

The debate about no-first-use is closely linked with the debate about the deterrent or war-fighting functions of nuclear weapons. Those who consider that nuclear weapons can be used for fighting wars are obviously not prepared to accept the situation in which the employment of these weapons depends on their prior use by an adversary.

The implication of a no-first-use posture is clear. With such a posture, the sole function of nuclear weapons is to act as a deterrent to their use by another nation. If that is the case, then substantial changes should follow in the composition and deployment of nuclear forces. The requirement of deterrence is simply that it should be possible to inflict unacceptable damage on any nation which resorts first to nuclear weapons. Many of the recent technological developments in

15

nuclear weaponry are seen to be unnecessary for this purpose. There is no point in developing nuclear weapons for counterforce purposes, if the sole function of these weapons is deterrence. The role of tactical nuclear weapons is also a war-fighting rather than a deterrent role. It would follow, therefore, that mutual declarations of no-first-use by the nuclear powers should be accompanied by substantial changes in nuclear armaments.

III. Conclusions

A policy of no-first-use of nuclear weapons has implications across the entire range of such weapons, from short-range battlefield to intercontinental strategic systems. It is intimately linked with conventional force postures, and bears on naval force planning too. It has relevance for any part of the world where nuclear weapons are assigned military roles. Primarily, however, no-first-use is still a European matter, and the possible first use of tactical nuclear weapons is the main issue. It is pertinent to both alliances, and has become a major subject of debate and controversy within NATO.

Limited nuclear war

Basic to any consideration of the advantages and disadvantages of no-first-use policies is the notion of limited nuclear war.

There are two thresholds of significance in relation to nuclear war. The first one, commonly referred to as 'the nuclear threshold', constitutes the distinction between conventional and nuclear means of warfare. To some extent, the existence of cluster bombs, fuel–air explosives and conventional area munitions which have mass destruction effects may erode this threshold. So may new nuclear weapons designed to cause less collateral damage than weapons of older type. Lethal chemical weapons—also inherently indiscriminate—may weaken the distinction even further, should they become fully integrated in the major powers' force structures. Nevertheless, a decision to authorize the first use of nuclear weapons, breaking a 40-year practice of non-use, would be a hard decision to make.

The second threshold is a geographical one and follows the borders of the nuclear powers. Should an armed confrontation in Europe escalate into nuclear war, both superpowers would, of course, do their best to keep their own territories out of it. The logic of this is overwhelming; it is not necessary to read public statements or war manuals to know that this is so. What applies to Europe applies to an even greater extent to south-west Asia, Korea and other parts of the world where the use of ruclear weapons might be contemplated; there, the superpowers have less at stake than in Europe and, therefore, less reason to risk devastation of their homelands. This is of course not to say that a nuclear war in Europe would actually be so confined—only that the USA and the USSR would try to confine it in this way. Technological mishaps, a chaotic battlefield, the

16

breakdown of command, control, communications and intelligence (C^3I) facilities and human behaviour under extreme stress must raise doubts as to whether they would succeed.

European interests

If the nuclear threshold is crossed, a selective use of nuclear weapons in the battle area, or observance of firebreaks to limit collateral damage, are extremely hard to imagine.

Nuclear warfighting can in no way be portrayed as meaningful defence. The moment NATO's first-use policy were to be carried into effect, it would have failed, because from then on, Europe would be subject to destruction rather than defence. There are bound to be doubts about the willingness of the west European leaders to commit national suicide. Indeed, several retired chiefs of the British defence staff have indicated that under no circumstances would they recommend that NATO should initiate the use of nuclear weapons.[24]

It is not surprising, therefore, that NATO has never agreed on guidelines for a follow-on action in case an initial use does not succeed in persuading the adversary to stop hostilities. Short-range or battlefield nuclear weapons, deployed for use in the early stages of a nuclear war, seem not to be prescribed in SACEUR's nuclear operation plan. Instead, it would be for the corps commanders to propose pre-packaged options resembling those rehearsed in exercises, in accordance with the US Army Manual on tactical nuclear operations. A corps package might consist of 100–200 warheads: "Each package must contain nuclear weapons sufficient to alter the tactical situation decisively and to accomplish the mission".[25] The fact that NATO has endorsed a policy of first use of nuclear weapons without ever agreeing on how to continue employing them in a way that would make military sense and be politically acceptable testifies to the half-hearted nature of this endorsement.

The first-use doctrine is therefore a constant source of uneasiness within the Alliance, especially when East–West tension increases, and with it the risk of war. Then, its flawed nature becomes exposed, and Alliance relations become strained. Precisely when the need for Alliance cohesion and determination is most important, public protest becomes more vocal and political divisions come to the surface. When there is a danger of war, NATO's threat to cross the nuclear threshold deters people in the West as much as it deters the WTO. Threatening first use is, moreover, an invitation to the opponent not to wait until that happens, but to strike first.

US concerns

In the fog of war, under extreme stress and time pressure, the USA may overrule European anxieties and resort to nuclear warfighting. In practice, European states hardly have any right of veto. They may not even be consulted. The Athens guidelines only prescribe consultations "time and circumstances permitting".[26]

Nuclear war is probably easier to contemplate if it is to be fought on the territory of third parties. The stronger the belief that it can be so limited, the greater the likelihood that it will be initiated.

However, the fear that any use of nuclear weapons would escalate into all-out nuclear war has not subsided. In the words of former US Secretary of Defense Robert McNamara "...NATO has not found it possible to develop plans...which would both assure a clear advantage to the alliance and at the same time avoid the very high risk of escalating to all-out nuclear war".[27] Two factors make it more difficult for the USA to initiate the use of nuclear weapons than it would have been 20 years ago, or before the doctrine of flexible response was proclaimed. First, the Soviet Union now has more options, greater flexibility and greater fire power for nuclear warfighting in Europe. This circumstance makes it less likely that the use of nuclear weapons would yield military advantages, or stop short of further escalation. Second, given the devastation that surviving Soviet forces could inflict on the United States, the US president cannot really be expected to initiate a strategic strike against the USSR in defence of western Europe. The ultimate sanction of the flexible response strategy has lost its credibility. As the Soviet Union achieved parity in strategic forces, the last rung of the escalation ladder was, in effect, removed. The credibility of the first use doctrine is therefore questionable also when seen from the US end of the Alliance.

The unity of the Western Alliance

There is a basic conflict of security interests between the USA and its European allies, the USA wanting to ensure that a war which starts in Europe should be limited to Europe, and the allies wanting to connect the European battle with US central strategic forces. However, no technological fix can restore the coupling between NATO forces in Europe and US strategic forces. Forward-based cruise and Pershing missiles cannot do that. Neither is it realistic to expect that enormous investments in US strategic weaponry can re-establish an edge over the Soviet Union of such a kind or magnitude that the threat of escalation would once again be credible. The nuclear umbrella, defined as US willingness to use nuclear weapons against the Soviet Union for the defence of western Europe, is gone. In the world of today, there are five or six nuclear umbrellas. They cover the five or six nuclear weapon states and no more.

It has been argued that adoption of a no-first-use policy would endanger the unity of the Western Alliance. In reality, such a policy would bring NATO's nuclear doctrine more in line with that of the United States. In their bilateral relationship, the superpowers have taken due account of the fact that first use of nuclear weapons is likely to trigger retaliation in kind, and probably amount to nuclear holocaust for both. Because of the vulnerability of both countries, there exists a tacit understanding that neither of them would strike first (although the understanding may be gradually undermined by the procurement of systems designed to destroy the retaliatory forces of the adversary). The same compelling logic applies to the two parts of Europe. First use of nuclear weapons is likely to lead to unacceptable destruction for both, and western Europe is as important to Europeans as the United States is to Americans. Self-preservation is equally important to both.

The force posture

There is a considerable discrepancy between the security interests of NATO and its force posture. Large stocks of nuclear arms are deployed near the East–West border and are commingled with conventional munitions. This situation is not compatible with the caution and prudence that NATO's decision-making councils are supposed to exercise at the outbreak of hostilities and in the early phases of a war.

After the withdrawal of the 1 000 nuclear weapons mentioned in the NATO Council communiqué of 12 December 1979, the distribution of weapons in major system categories was reported to be as follows:

Bombs to be delivered by aircraft	1 069
Artillery shells (155-mm and 203-mm)	2 000
Missiles: Pershing IA	270
Lance and Honest John	910
Air defence and atomic demolition mines	1 750
Total	5 999

Source: North Atlantic Assembly's Special Committee on Nuclear Weapons in Europe, *Second Interim Report on Nuclear Weapons,* Report to the Committee on Foreign Relations, US Senate, 98th Congress, 1st session (US Government Printing Office, Washington, D.C., 1983), p. 59.

Atomic demolition mines would have to be used at the very beginning of a conflict, to avoid being overrun, captured or destroyed by the enemy. Much the same goes for the nuclear-tipped air defence systems (Nike Hercules). These elements of the nuclear arsenal indicate not only the inevitability of early use, but also tend to negate the very essence of the strategy of flexible response. For they would be used before NATO's ability to stop a conventional attack by conventional means had been tested, whereas the strategy of flexible response prescribes resort to nuclear weapons only when conventional forces face a defeat.

One-third of the west European nuclear arsenal consists of artillery shells stored at a few sites close to the East–West border, ready to be coupled during a crisis or war to guns deployed near that border. Obviously, large numbers of nuclear weapons near the front line constitute attractive targets before they have been moved out of the depots, or before the authority has been given to field commanders to use them. Some observers agree that a pre-emptive attack on these inventories would be very likely, and claim that NATO has implicitly accepted the loss of many of them.[28] Others stress that for fear of seeing them overrun, the United States would permit the use of nuclear munitions almost as soon as war broke out, disregarding Alliance authorization procedures. Neither outcome seems comforting. A large nuclear artillery inventory invites pre-emption. The alternative—the early use of that inventory to avoid pre-emption—would start a nuclear war, a wholly unacceptable risk.

The commingling of nuclear and conventional forces also makes the early use of nuclear weapons more likely. If the conventional battle is even and the outcome remains uncertain, a field commander, guided by the principles of flexible response, might withhold the use of dual-capable (that is, both conventional and nuclear) systems, in spite of the fact that maximum conventional strength is needed. He may do this because he expects an escalation to nuclear war. The integration of conventional and nuclear weapons into an operational military doctrine reduces conventional strength in other ways as well. Armed forces that exercise under the assumption that nuclear warfare will be initiated, either by themselves or by the opponent, are less prepared for a war confined exclusively to conventional means. Forces trained to disperse in the expectation of the use of nuclear weapons by the adversary may be unprepared to regroup if that expectation is not fulfilled. There is thus a danger that a presumed conventional inferiority may become a self-fulfilling prophecy.

Some NATO countries have already decided to replace the Nike Hercules nuclear systems with conventionally tipped Patriot air-defence missiles.[29] NATO has announced the withdrawal of 1 400 nuclear weapons from Europe over the coming five to six years, including atomic demolition mines and Nike Hercules munitions. With the introduction of new intermediate-range theatre forces, further nuclear weapons are to be removed on a one-to-one replacement basis. All these measures may indicate that NATO's nuclear posture is slowly moving towards no-early-use. However, much greater changes than this are needed for a binding and credible no-first-use commitment.

Approaches to the implementation of a no-first-use commitment

If backed by strong political will, a declared commitment not to be the first to use nuclear weapons could be a powerful directive for military force planners to restructure their defences. Having announced its no-first-use pledge in 1982, the Soviet Union hinted that there would be visible consequences for all to see. However, such consequences still remain to be identified. The United States has asserted, and the Soviet Union has not denied, that nuclear weapons are stored in east European countries.[30] This puts the value of the Soviet commitment in doubt. The subsequent deployments in the GDR and Czechoslovakia of theatre nuclear weapons further weaken the credibility of this commitment. Any declaration which raises expectations that are not matched by subsequent changes in military force structure is bound to be discredited. There is, therefore, an argument for starting at the other end, by making the force posture compatible with a no-first-use stance, which is then declared after the force posture has been changed.

Thus NATO could insert a new provision into its long-term defence plan, committing the organization to make its force posture compatible with a

20

declaration of no-first-use by the end of the five-year planning period.

One important thing that has to be done to bring about a change of this kind is the withdrawal of tactical nuclear weapons which are now in or near potential combat zones. Here, then, is the link between two central propositions in the current debate concerning nuclear weapons in Europe—disengagement zones and a no-first-use commitment.[31]

The disengagement zone represents a *hardware* approach to raising the nuclear threshold. If nuclear weapons were removed from specified areas, military doctrines would obviously have to place less emphasis on the early use of nuclear weapons. A *software* approach would be to de-emphasize the early use of nuclear weapons by rewriting military doctrines and manuals. The two approaches could complement each other.

Clearly, the United States would have to change its force configuration before making no-first-use part of its policy. The validity of the present Soviet no-first-use declaration will also depend on whether concrete measures are taken to assure its compatibility with the WTO force posture. The battlefield nuclear weapon-free zone idea could be an appropriate way to make progress in this matter. Even a modest withdrawal of nuclear weapons—for instance, along the lines suggested in 1982 by the International Commission for Disarmament and Security Issues—would raise the nuclear threshold significantly.[32] It would reduce the danger of inadvertent escalation to nuclear war and, in particular, minimize the 'use them or lose them' dilemma, that is, the choice between firing the weapons or abandoning them to the enemy. Politically, it would provide some greatly needed mutual confidence. A disengagement zone in central Europe could, moreover, be considered in conjunction with the proposals for nuclear weapon-free zones in northern and southern Europe.

To reduce even further the likelihood of first use, the measures outlined above could be subsequently supplemented by deployment limitations on nuclear weapons in areas adjacent to the disengagement zone, preferably by removing nuclear weapons from all European states which do not themselves possess such weapons.[33]

No-first-use and conventional forces

A policy of abstention from the first use of nuclear weapons implies that states will retain or acquire a capability to repel conventional aggression with conventional weapons. Accordingly, no-first-use also presupposes some East–West agreement on conventional forces in Europe, and/or unilateral changes of conventional defences.

No one can credibly claim to know what the actual relationship of conventional force is or what course a conventional war in Europe could take. A dominant perception in Western political and military establishments is that the WTO has the upper edge, even though NATO is superior in command, communications and control, electronic warfare capability, precision-guided munitions, and surveillance. WTO officials do not share this view, but they seem reasonably confident in the capabilities of their own conventional forces.

The link between a nuclear no-first-use policy and changes in conventional force structure is a complex issue which can be approached in a variety of ways. Basically, there are three options: unilateral conventional rearmament, non-provocative defence, and East–West arms reduction. Each of these is considered in turn.

Throughout its history NATO has, from time to time, decided to attempt to redress perceived imbalances in its conventional military position *vis-à-vis* the WTO. One such decision was that of May 1977, at the initiative of President Carter. A Long Term Defence Programme was adopted, and the members of NATO set for themselves a target increase in military expenditure of 3 per cent per year in real terms.[34] In the development of this programme there was increasing stress on exploiting the NATO countries' differential advantage in military technology. Thus the guidance to the defence planners in 1977 stated that efficient application of modern technology, while not offering any inexpensive solutions, can provide opportunities, if applied through co-operative and timely efforts, for substantial improvement in the deterrent and defence capabilities of the Alliance.[35] This theme has been reiterated frequently in the period since then. Indeed there have been significant advances in the sophistication of conventional weaponry in recent years, mainly due to the 'electronic revolution', with break-throughs in real-time battlefield surveillance/target acquisition and 'fire-and-forget' munitions.

NATO's Commander-in-Chief, General Bernard Rogers, has indeed suggested that if NATO countries were prepared to increase their spending sufficiently on the new conventional military technology, NATO could at least move towards 'no-early-use'—that is, a military posture in which the resort to nuclear weapons could come much later than is at present envisaged. His suggested rate of increase in military spending, to achieve this objective, is one of 4 per cent per year in real terms.[36] The Rogers Plan includes the so-called Follow-On Force Attack (FOFA), which aims to influence the front-line battle by striking fixed targets, such as military installations or bridges, deep inside eastern Europe or the western part of the Soviet Union.[37]

Adoption of the deep-strike concept would almost certainly bring about a competitive East–West buildup of conventional arms; for the problem with measures of this kind is that they are bound to generate countermeasures. A perceived military imbalance can only be corrected if the potential adversary permits it. If he does not, and simply increases his own military spending *pari passu*, the imbalance persists at a higher level of military deployment on both sides.

This leads to the second possibility, that of strengthening the conventional defences in such a way that the changes do not appear as provocative or offensive to the other side.

A nation—or an alliance—with a non-provocative defence stance is one which is perceived as being incapable of seizing and holding the territory of other nations or of inflicting serious damage on the people or assets of another nation.[38]

22

Single elements of the posture may (unavoidably) have offensive connotations, but need not detract significantly from the overall defensive character of the posture.

There is an obvious link between the concept of a non-provocative defence structure, and the idea of disengagement zones, from which not only nuclear weapons but also major conventional systems suitable for offensive use are withdrawn. Thus, tanks, medium and heavy conventional and dual-capable artillery, as well as multiple-rocket launchers and bridging equipment, would have to be removed, leaving only weapons which are unsuitable for offensive strikes. Such disengagement would render an offensive operation difficult. A network of small military units, armed with light precision-guided munitions for anti-armour and anti-aircraft use, and a fortified border, would further enhance the chances of a successful defence.

However, the complexities of negotiating an arrangement extending both east and west of the dividing line in Europe may justify a second-best solution—*unilateral* adoption of a less provocative defence posture—on the assumption that even this would create a more tenable situation than that which obtains today.

The third possible way of preparing for a no-first-use stance—and undoubtedly the most desirable one—would be to achieve a mutually accepted balance of conventional forces by lowering the level of arms.

Achieving balance does not necessarily mean matching the other side man for man, or establishing direct parity, quantitatively or qualitatively, in all categories of arms. States have placed different emphasis on various components of their forces due to geographic and economic dissimilarities, as well as differences in technology, in military structure and in defence arrangements. What matters is an equilibrium between the overall military potential of the opposing parties. However, it would be important to remove the most glaring discrepancies in weapon inventories, especially those that could give rise to misapprehensions that an attack by an adversary might be successful. It would be equally essential to agree on such force deployment patterns, as well as constraints on certain military activities, that would minimize the risk of a surprise attack. To generate confidence, the balance must be generally seen to be stable. An assurance is also needed that the situation would not suddenly change in favour of one side. Therefore, there must be a negotiated legal commitment to hold the forces down to agreed levels, including provisions to check compliance.

Summary

Whereas the first use of nuclear weapons for aggression is recognized as being unambiguously illegal, the first use of such weapons for defence remains a moot issue. Our argument is that the right to self-defence is not unlimited, that it is restricted by the dictates of humanity, by the general principles of international law, and by specific international treaty obligations. Indeed, whatever the purpose, one cannot justify the use of weapons which would not only indiscriminately destroy enemy forces and population, but also would seriously injure the defended people themselves, as well as the neutrals not involved in the conflict. The doctrine which accepts the possibility of the first use of nuclear weapons is now questioned by leading religious, political and military authorities.

However, a mere no-first-use declaration would not suffice to provide a dependable defence. To be meaningful, it would have to be accompanied—or preferably preceded—by changes in the deployment of both nuclear and conventional forces.

In the nuclear field, the removal of battlefield nuclear weapons from areas adjacent to the East–West border in Europe would be an obvious first step. It could be followed by the removal of nuclear weapons from the territories of all European countries which do not themselves possess them.

In the conventional field, there are two possibilities for removing the perceived discrepancies in military strength—which have so far been referred to in justifying the first-use doctrine—without setting off a new arms race. One possibility is to achieve a mutually acceptable balance of forces by lowering the level of arms. Another is to construct a system of 'non-provocative' defence, starting with a properly constituted disengagement zone. The two approaches could be combined with each other.

There is a strong case for Western preparation for a no-first-use commitment and for the Soviet Union's demonstration—through military deployment—of the seriousness of its declared intent never to be the first to use nuclear weapons. NATO could insert a new provision into its long-term defence plan, committing the Organization to make its force posture compatible with a future policy of no-first-use to be declared, say, by the end of the five-year planning period. The Soviet Union could refrain from introducing into eastern Europe tactical nuclear missiles which have the characteristics of first-use weapons. Such moves would go at least some way towards allaying the fears of the very large number of people who are now deeply concerned about the state of East–West relations.

Notes and References

[1] *The Church and the Bomb, The General Synod Debate*, February 1983 (CIO Publishing, London, 1983), p. 39.
[2] Resolution of the Church of Scotland, quoted in the Ecumenical Press Service, 25 June 1983.
[3] Resolution of a four-day gathering of church leaders from 60 countries, meeting in Uppsala, Sweden, quoted in the Ecumenical Press Service, 1 May 1983.
[4] *The Challenge of Peace: God's Promise and Our Response*, A Pastoral Letter on War and Peace, 3 May 1983, National Conference of Catholic Bishops (United States Catholic Conference, Washington, D.C., 1983).
[5] *The Challenge of Peace: God's Promise and Our Response* (note 4), pp. iii and iv.
[6] *The Challenge of Peace: God's Promise and Our Response* (note 4), p. 4.
[7] *The Times*, London, 17 November 1983, p. 12.
[8] *Le Matin*, 24 March 1983: "P. Gérard Debois, Secrétaire du Conseil Permanent de l'Episcopat Français ('une sorte de premier ministre catholique') estimait qu'un débat sur le nucléaire militaire serait 'inimaginable' dans notre pays".

[9] Ecumenical Press Service, 25 June 1983.
[10] *Disarmament Campaign*, No. 27, November 1983, p. 6.
[11] *The Church and the Bomb* (note 1), p. 67.
[12] See, for example, *Air Force Magazine*, Vol. 61, No. 1, January 1983, p. 67; and *Strategic Review*, Vol. 11, No. 3, Summer 1983, p. 43.
[13] Bouscaren, A. T., 'Just war, nuclear arms and the Catholic bishops', *Strategic Review*, Vol. 11, No. 3, Summer 1983, pp. 43–50.
[14] van Voorit, L. B., 'The churches and nuclear deterrence', *Foreign Affairs*, Vol. 61, No. 4, Spring 1983, p. 847.
[15] van Voorit, L. B. (note 14), pp. 846–47.
[16] Alternative Defence Commission, *Defence Without the Bomb* (Taylor & Francis, London, 1983), pp. 45–49.
[17] Excerpts from the Protocol are reproduced in Goldblat, J., *Agreements for Arms Control*, SIPRI (Taylor & Francis, London, 1982).
[18] UN General Assembly Resolution 1(I), 24 January 1946.
[19] UN General Assembly Resolution 1653 (XVI), 24 November 1961.
[20] UN General Assembly Resolution 1936 (XXVII), 29 November 1972.
[21] UN General Assembly Resolution 38/73, 15 December 1983.
[22] UN General Assembly Resolution 38/75, 15 December 1983.
[23] UN document A/S-12/PV. 12, 8 June 1982.
[24] A speech by Admiral of the Fleet Earl Mountbatten of Burma on the occasion of the award of the Louise Weiss Foundation Prize to SIPRI at Strasbourg, 11 May 1979, p. 3; Lord Carver in a speech for the Council on Arms Control, Second Annual Lecture, London, 9 November 1983. Admiral of the Fleet and Chairman of the Military Committee of NATO Lord Hill-Norton and Marshall of the British Air Force Lord Cameron of Dalhousie have expressed similar views.
[25] *Field Manual 100-5*, US Department of the Army, 1982.
[26] *The Second Interim Report on Nuclear Weapons in Europe*, A Report to the SFRC (US Government Printing Office, Washington, D.C., January 1983). P. 8, section 27 reads: "Furthermore, given the awesome nature of the decision to use nuclear weapons, few experts believe that the NATO political consultation process could possibly function effectively in time of crisis. (8)."
P. 8, note 8 reads: "With regard to the political consultation process, the Athens Guidelines of 1963 state that the United States will consult with its Allies on the use of tactical nuclear weapons 'time and circumstances permitting'. The US President retains the right to use American nuclear weapons without prior consultation."
[27] McNamara, R. S., "The military role of nuclear weapons: perceptions and misperceptions", *Foreign Affairs*, Vol. 62, No. 1, Fall 1983, p. 69.
[28] See, for example, Sigal, L. V., "No first use and NATO's nuclear posture", in Steinbruner, J. and Sigal, L. V. (eds), *Alliance Security: NATO and the No-First-Use Questions* (The Brookings Institution, Washington, D.C., 1983).
[29] *International Defense Digest*, Vol. 16, No. 11, 1983, pp. 1533–35.
[30] Stern: "Hat die Sowjetunion ausserhalb ihres eigenen Territoriums Atomwaffen gelagert?", Tscherwow: "Darauf eine klare Antwort: Überall, wo ausserhalb der Sowjetunion unsere Divisionen stehen, besitzen die Raketeneinheiten der betreffenden Divisionen Atomwaffen taktischer Reichweite von etwa 100 Kilometern. Aber genauso eindeutig sage ich: Ausserhalb unseres Staatsgebietes gibt es keine sowjetischen Mittelstreckenraketen oder strategischen Nuklearwaffen." Interview with General Nikolaj Tscherwow by the West German magazine *Stern*, 20 October 1983.

31 For further elaboration, see Lodgaard, S. and Thee, M. (eds), *Nuclear Disengagement in Europe*, SIPRI (Taylor & Francis, London, 1983).

32 *Common Security. A Programme for Disarmament*, the Report of the Independent Commission on Disarmament and Security Issues under the Chairmanship of Olof Palme (Pan Books, London, 1982).

33 See Bahr, E., Annex Two to *Common Security* (note 32).

34 *NATO Review*, Vol. 25, No. 3, June 1977, pp. 3–5, 20–27.

35 *NATO Review* (note 34), p. 26.

36 *Atlantic News*, No. 1437, 7 July 1982, p. 2.

37 Development of the key concept of attacking WTO follow-on forces began at SHAPE in late 1979 and was approved by the Military Committee in October 1981. See *Atlantic News*, No. 1461, 22 October 1982, p. 2 and No. 1556, 21 September 1983, pp. 2–3.

There are a number of variations on this theme of attacking the enemy behind the front line. A deep-strike concept supported by the Office of the US Secretary of Defense would also involve attacks on mobile military functions, probably including mobile theatre nuclear weapons, at the same range as FOFA.

The Air-Land battle concept of the US Army proposes the use not only of conventional weapons, but also of theatre nuclear and chemical weapons, at ranges well in excess of 150 km. A good introductory article is that of Hanne, W. G., "Air-Land Battle—doctrine not dogma", *International Defense Review*, Vol. 16, No. 8, 1983, pp. 1035–40. Note the difference between the present Air-Land doctrine and the more futuristic and controversial Air-Land Battle 2000 concept. On the latter, see TRADOC, *Air-Land Battle 2000* (Fort Monroe, VA, 1982).

38 Afheldt, H., *Defensive Verteidigung*, Rororo Aktuell No. 5345 (Rowohlt Verlag, Reinbek–Hamburg, 1983).

Part II
No-first-use—
main arguments for and against

Nuclear weapons and the Atlantic Alliance

McGeorge Bundy, George F. Kennan, Robert S. McNamara and Gerard Smith[1]
Reprinted by permission of Foreign Affairs, Spring 1982. Copyright 1982 by the Council on Foreign Relations, Inc.

We are four Americans who have been concerned over many years with the relation between nuclear weapons and the peace and freedom of the members of the Atlantic Alliance. Having learned that each of us separately has been coming to hold new views on this hard but vital question, we decided to see how far our thoughts, and the lessons of our varied experiences, could be put together; the essay that follows is the result. It argues that a new policy can bring great benefits, but it aims to start a discussion, not to end it.

For 33 years now, the Atlantic Alliance has relied on the asserted readiness of the United States to use nuclear weapons if necessary to repel aggression from the East. Initially, indeed, it was widely thought (notably by such great and different men as Winston Churchill and Niels Bohr) that the basic military balance in Europe was between American atomic bombs and the massive conventional forces of the Soviet Union. But the first Soviet explosion, in August 1949, ended the American monopoly only one month after the Senate approved the North Atlantic Treaty, and in 1950 communist aggression in Korea produced new Allied attention to the defense of Europe.

The "crude" atomic bombs of the 1940s have been followed in both countries by a fantastic proliferation of weapons and delivery systems, so that today the two parts of a still-divided Europe are targeted by many thousands of warheads both in the area and outside it. Within the Alliance, France and Britain have developed thermonuclear forces which are enormous compared to what the United States had at the beginning, although small by comparison with the present deployments of the superpowers. Doctrine has succeeded doctrine, from "balanced collective forces" to "massive retaliation" to "mutual assured destruction" to "flexible response" and the "seamless web." Throughout these transformations, most of them occasioned at least in part by changes in the Western view of Soviet capabilities, both deployments and doctrines have been intended to deter Soviet aggression and keep the peace by maintaining a credible connection between any large-scale assault, whether conventional or nuclear, and the engagement of the strategic nuclear forces of the United States.

A major element in every doctrine has been that the United States has asserted its willingness to be the first—has indeed made plans to be the first if necessary—to use nuclear weapons to defend against aggression in Europe. It is this element that needs re-examination now. Both its cost to the coherence of the Alliance and its threat to the safety of the world are rising while its deterrent credibility declines.

This policy was first established when the American nuclear advantage was overwhelming, but that advantage has long since gone and cannot be recaptured. As early as the 1950s it was recognized by both Prime Minister Churchill and President Eisenhower that the nuclear strength of both sides was becoming so great that a nuclear war would be a ghastly catastrophe for all concerned. The following decades have only confirmed and intensified that reality. The time has come for careful study of the ways and means of moving to a new Alliance policy and doctrine: that nuclear weapons will not be used unless an aggressor should use them first.

II

The disarray that currently besets the nuclear policy and practices of the Alliance is obvious. Governments and their representatives have maintained an appearance of unity as they persist in their support of the two-track decision of December 1979, under which 572 new American missiles of intermediate range are to be placed in Europe unless a satisfactory agreement on the limitation of such weapons can be reached in the negotiations between the United States and the Soviet Union that began last November. But behind this united front there are divisive debates, especially in countries where the new weapons are to be deployed.

The arguments put forward by advocates of these deployments contain troubling variations. The simplest and intuitively the most persuasive claim is that these new weapons are needed as a counter to the new Soviet SS-20 missiles; it may be a recognition of the surface attractiveness of this position that underlies President Reagan's striking—but probably not negotiable—proposal that if all the SS-20s are dismantled the planned deployments will be cancelled. Other officials have a quite different argument, that without new and survivable American weapons which can reach Russia from Western Europe there can be no confidence that the strategic forces of the United States will remain committed to the defense of Western Europe; on this argument the new missiles are needed to make it more likely that any war in Europe would bring nuclear warheads on the Soviet Union and thus deter the aggressor in the first place. This argument is logically distinct from any concern about the Soviet SS-20s, and it probably explains the ill-concealed hope of some planners that the Reagan proposal will be rejected. Such varied justifications cast considerable doubt on the real purpose of the proposed deployment.

An equally disturbing phenomenon is the gradual shift in the balance of argument that has occurred since the need to address the problem was first asserted in

1977. Then the expression of need was European, and in the first instance German; the emerging parity of long-range strategic systems was asserted to create a need for a balance at less than intercontinental levels. The American interest developed relatively slowly, but because these were to be American missiles, American planners took the lead as the proposal was worked out. It has also served Soviet purposes to concentrate on the American role. A similar focus has been chosen by many leaders of the new movement for nuclear disarmament in Europe. And now there are American voices, some in the executive branch, talking as if European acceptance of these new missiles were some sort of test of European loyalty to the Alliance. Meanwhile some of those in Europe who remain publicly committed to both tracks of the 1979 agreement are clearly hoping that the day of deployment will never arrive. When the very origins of a new proposal become the source of irritated argument among allies—"You started it!"—something is badly wrong in our common understanding.

A still more severe instance of disarray, one which has occurred under both President Carter and President Reagan, relates to the so-called neutron bomb, a weapon designed to meet the threat of Soviet tanks. American military planners, authorized by doctrine to think in terms of early battlefield use of nuclear weapons, naturally want more "up-to-date" weapons than those they have now; it is known that thousands of the aging short-range nuclear weapons now in Europe are hard to use effectively. Yet to a great many Europeans the neutron bomb suggests, however unfairly, that the Americans are preparing to fight a "limited" nuclear war on their soil. Moreover neither weapons designers nor the Pentagon officials they have persuaded seem to have understood the intense and special revulsion that is associated with killing by "enhanced radiation."

All these recent distempers have a deeper cause. They are rooted in the fact that the evolution of essentially equivalent and enormously excessive nuclear weapons systems both in the Soviet Union and in the Atlantic Alliance has aroused new concern about the dangers of all forms of nuclear war. The profusion of these systems, on both sides, has made it more difficult than ever to construct rational plans for any first use of these weapons by anyone.

This problem is more acute than before, but it is not new. Even in the 1950s, a time that is often mistakenly perceived as one of effortless American superiority, the prospect of any actual use of tactical weapons was properly terrifying to Europeans and to more than a few Americans. Military plans for such use remained both deeply secret and highly hypothetical; the coherence of the Alliance was maintained by general neglect of such scenarios, not by sedulous public discussion. In the 1960s there was a prolonged and stressful effort to address the problem of theater-range weapons, but agreement on new forces and plans for their use proved elusive. Eventually the proposal for a multilateral force (MLF) was replaced by the assignment of American Polaris submarines to NATO, and by the creation in Brussels of an inter-allied Nuclear Planning Group. Little else was accomplished. In both decades the Alliance kept itself together more by mutual political confidence than by plausible nuclear war-fighting plans.

Although the first years of the 1970s produced a welcome if oversold détente, complacency soon began to fade. The Nixon Administration, rather quietly, raised the question about the long-run credibility of the American nuclear deterrent that was to be elaborated by Henry Kissinger in 1979 at a meeting in Brussels. Further impetus to both new doctrine and new deployments came during the Ford and Carter Administrations, but each public statement, however careful and qualified, only increased European apprehensions. The purpose of both Administrations was to reinforce deterrence, but the result has been to increase fear of nuclear war, and even of Americans as its possible initiators. Intended as contributions to both rationality and credibility, these excursions into the theory of limited nuclear war have been counterproductive in Europe.

Yet it was not wrong to raise these matters. Questions that were answered largely by silence in the 1950s and 1960s cannot be so handled in the 1980s. The problem was not in the fact that the questions were raised, but in the way they seemed to be answered.

It is time to recognize that no one has ever succeeded in advancing any persuasive reason to believe that any use of nuclear weapons, even on the smallest scale, could reliably be expected to remain limited. Every serious analysis and every military exercise, for over 25 years, has demonstrated that even the most restrained battlefield use would be enormously destructive to civilian life and property. There is no way for anyone to have any confidence that such a nuclear action will not lead to further and more devastating exchanges. Any use of nuclear weapons in Europe, by the Alliance or against it, carries with it a high and inescapable risk of escalation into the general nuclear war which would bring ruin to all and victory to none.

The one clearly definable firebreak against the worldwide disaster of general nuclear war is the one that stands between all other kinds of conflict and any use whatsoever of nuclear weapons. To keep that firebreak wide and strong is in the deepest interest of all mankind. In retrospect, indeed, it is remarkable that this country has not responded to this reality more quickly. Given the appalling consequences of even the most limited use of nuclear weapons and the total impossibility for both sides of any guarantee against unlimited escalation, there must be the gravest doubt about the wisdom of a policy which asserts the effectiveness of any first use of nuclear weapons by either side. So it seems timely to consider the possibilities, the requirements, the difficulties, and the advantages of a policy of no-first-use.

III

The largest question presented by any proposal for an Allied policy of no-first-use is that of its impact on the effectiveness of NATO's deterrent posture on the central front. In spite of the doubts that are created by any honest look at the probable consequences of resort to a first nuclear strike of any kind, it should be remembered that there were strong reasons for the creation of the American nuclear umbrella over NATO. The original American pledge, expressed in Article

5 of the Treaty, was understood to be a nuclear guarantee. It was extended at a time when only a conventional Soviet threat existed, so a readiness for first use was plainly implied from the beginning. To modify that guarantee now, even in the light of all that has happened since, would be a major change in the assumptions of the Alliance, and no such change should be made without the most careful exploration of its implications.

In such an exploration the role of the Federal Republic of Germany must be central. Americans too easily forget what the people of the Federal Republic never can: that their position is triply exposed in a fashion unique among the large industrial democracies. They do not have nuclear weapons; they share a long common boundary with the Soviet empire; in any conflict on the central front their land would be the first battleground. None of these conditions can be changed, and together they present a formidable challenge.

Having decisively rejected a policy of neutrality, the Federal Republic has necessarily relied on the nuclear protection of the United States, and we Americans should recognize that this relationship is not a favor we are doing our German friends, but the best available solution of a common problem. Both nations believe that the Federal Republic must be defended; both believe that the Federal Republic must not have nuclear weapons of its own; both believe that nuclear guarantees *of some sort* are essential; and both believe that only the United States can provide those guarantees in persuasively deterrent peace-keeping form.

The uniqueness of the West German position can be readily demonstrated by comparing it with those of France and the United Kingdom. These two nations have distance, and in one case water, between them and the armies of the Soviet Union; they also have nuclear weapons. While those weapons may contribute something to the common strength of the Alliance, their main role is to underpin a residual national self-reliance, expressed in different ways at different times by different governments, which sets both Britain and France apart from the Federal Republic. They are set apart from the United States too, in that no other nation depends on them to use their nuclear weapons otherwise than in their own ultimate self-defense.

The quite special character of the nuclear relationship between the Federal Republic and the United States is a most powerful reason for defining that relationship with great care. It is rare for one major nation to depend entirely on another for a form of strength that is vital to its survival. It is unprecedented for any nation, however powerful, to pledge itself to a course of action, in defense of another, that might entail its own nuclear devastation. A policy of no-first-use would not and should not imply an abandonment of this extraordinary guarantee—only its redefinition. It would still be necessary to be ready to reply with American nuclear weapons to any nuclear attack on the Federal Republic, and this commitment would in itself be sufficiently demanding to constitute a powerful demonstration that a policy of no-first-use would represent no abandonment of our German ally.

The German right to a voice in this question is not merely a matter of location, or even of dependence on an American nuclear guarantee. The people of the Federal Republic have demonstrated a steadfast dedication to peace, to collective defense, and to domestic political decency. The study here proposed should be responsive to their basic desires. It seems probable that they are like the rest of us in wishing most of all to have no war of any kind, but also to be able to defend the peace by forces that do not require the dreadful choice of nuclear escalation.

IV

While we believe that careful study will lead to a firm conclusion that it is time to move decisively toward a policy of no-first-use, it is obvious that any such policy would require a strengthened confidence in the adequacy of the conventional forces of the Alliance, above all the forces in place on the central front and those available for prompt reinforcement. It seems clear that the nations of the Alliance together can provide whatever forces are needed, and within realistic budgetary constraints, but it is a quite different question whether they can summon the necessary political will. Evidence from the history of the Alliance is mixed. There has been great progress in the conventional defenses of NATO in the 30 years since the 1952 Lisbon communiqué, but there have also been failures to meet force goals all along the way.

In each of the four nations which account for more than 90 percent of NATO's collective defense and a still higher proportion of its strength on the central front, there remain major unresolved political issues that critically affect contributions to conventional deterrence: for example, it can be asked what priority the United Kingdom gives to the British Army of the Rhine, what level of NATO-connected deployment can be accepted by France, what degree of German relative strength is acceptable to the Allies and fair to the Federal Republic itself, and whether we Americans have a durable and effective answer to our military manpower needs in the present all-volunteer active and reserve forces. These are the kinds of questions—and there are many more—that would require review and resolution in the course of reaching any final decision to move to a responsible policy of no-first-use.

There should also be an examination of the ways in which the concept of early use of nuclear weapons may have been built into existing forces, tactics, and general military expectations. To the degree that this has happened, there could be a dangerous gap right now between real capabilities and those which political leaders might wish to have in a time of crisis. Conversely there should be careful study of what a policy of no-first-use would require in those same terms. It seems more than likely that once the military leaders of the Alliance have learned to think and act steadily on this "conventional" assumption, their forces will be better instruments for stability in crises and for general deterrence, as well as for the maintenance of the nuclear firebreak so vital to us all.

No one should underestimate either the difficulty or the importance of the shift in military attitudes implied by a no-first-use policy. Although military commanders are well aware of the terrible dangers in any exchange of nuclear weapons, it is a strong military tradition to maintain that aggressive war, not the use of any one weapon, is the central evil. Many officers will be initially unenthusiastic about any formal policy that puts limits on their recourse to a weapon of apparently decisive power. Yet the basic argument for a no-first-use policy can be stated in strictly military terms: that any other course involves unacceptable risks to the national life that military forces exist to defend. The military officers of the Alliance can be expected to understand the force of this proposition, even if many of them do not initially agree with it. Moreover, there is every reason for confidence that they will loyally accept any policy that has the support of their governments and the peoples behind them, just as they have fully accepted the present arrangements under which the use of nuclear weapons, even in retaliation for a nuclear attack, requires advance and specific approval by the head of government.

An Allied posture of no-first-use would have one special effect that can be set forth in advance: it would draw new attention to the importance of maintaining and improving the specifically American conventional forces in Europe. The principal political difficulty in a policy of no-first-use is that it may be taken in Europe, and especially in the Federal Republic, as evidence of a reduced American interest in the Alliance and in effective overall deterrence. The argument here is exactly the opposite: that such a policy is the best one available for keeping the Alliance united and effective. Nonetheless the psychological realities of the relation between the Federal Republic and the United States are such that the only way to prevent corrosive German suspicion of American intentions, under a no-first-use regime, will be for Americans to accept for themselves an appropriate share in any new level of conventional effort that the policy may require.

Yet it would be wrong to make any hasty judgment that those new levels of effort must be excessively high. The subject is complex, and the more so because both technology and politics are changing. Precision-guided munitions, in technology, and the visible weakening of the military solidity of the Warsaw Pact, in politics, are only two examples of changes working to the advantage of the Alliance. Moreover there has been some tendency, over many years, to exaggerate the relative conventional strength of the U.S.S.R. and to underestimate Soviet awareness of the enormous costs and risks of any form of aggression against NATO.

Today there is literally no one who really knows what would be needed. Most of the measures routinely used in both official and private analyses are static and fragmentary. An especially arbitrary, if obviously convenient, measure of progress is that of spending levels. But it is political will, not budgetary pressure, that will be decisive. The value of greater safety from both nuclear and conventional danger is so great that even if careful analysis showed that the necessary conventional posture would require funding larger than the three-percent real increase that has been the common target of recent years, it would be the best bargain ever offered to the members of the Alliance.

Yet there is no need for crash programs, which always bring extra costs. The direction of the Allied effort will be more important than its velocity. The final establishment of a firm policy of no-first-use, in any case, will obviously require time. What is important today is to begin to move in this direction.

V

The concept of renouncing any first use of nuclear weapons should also be tested by careful review of the value of existing NATO plans for selective and limited use of nuclear weapons. While many scenarios for nuclear war-fighting are nonsensical, it must be recognized that cautious and sober senior officers have found it prudent to ask themselves what alternatives to defeat they could propose to their civilian superiors if a massive conventional Soviet attack seemed about to make a decisive breakthrough. This question has generated contingency plans for battlefield uses of small numbers of nuclear weapons which might prevent that particular disaster. It is hard to see how any such action could be taken without the most enormous risk of rapid and catastrophic escalation, but it is a fair challenge to a policy of no-first-use that it should be accompanied by a level of conventional strength that would make such plans unnecessary.

In the light of this difficulty it would be prudent to consider whether there is any acceptable policy short of no-first-use. One possible example is what might be called "no-*early*-first-use;" such a policy might leave open the option of some limited nuclear action to fend off a final large-scale conventional defeat, and by renunciation of any immediate first use and increased emphasis on conventional capabilities it might be thought to help somewhat in reducing current fears.

But the value of a clear and simple position would be great, especially in its effect on ourselves and our Allies. One trouble with exceptions is that they easily become rules. It seems much better that even the most responsible choice of even the most limited nuclear actions to prevent even the most imminent conventional disaster should be left out of authorized policy. What the Alliance needs most today is not the refinement of its nuclear options, but a clear-cut decision to avoid them as long as others do.

VI

Who should make the examination here proposed? The present American Administration has so far shown little interest in questions of this sort, and indeed a seeming callousness in some quarters in Washington toward nuclear dangers may be partly responsible for some of the recent unrest in Europe. But each of the four of us has served in Administrations which revised their early thoughts on nuclear weapons policy. James Byrnes learned the need to seek international control; John Foster Dulles stepped back somewhat from his early belief in massive retaliation; Dwight Eisenhower came to believe in the effort to ban nuclear tests which he at first thought dangerous; the Administration of John F. Kennedy (in which we all served) modified its early views on targeting doctrine; Lyndon Johnson shelved the proposed MLF when he decided it was causing more trouble than it was worth; and Richard Nixon agreed to narrow limits on anti-ballistic missiles whose large-scale deployment he had once thought indispensable. There were changes also in the Ford and Carter Administrations, and President Reagan has already adjusted his views on the usefulness of early arms control negotiations, even though we remain in a time of general stress between Washington and Moscow. No Administration should be held, and none should hold itself, to inflexible first positions on these extraordinarily difficult matters.

Nor does this question need to wait upon governments for study. The day is long past when public awe and governmental secrecy made nuclear policy a matter for only the most private executive determination. The questions presented by a policy of no-first-use must indeed be decided by governments, but they can and should be considered by citizens. In recent months strong private voices have been raised on both sides of the Atlantic on behalf of strengthened conventional forces. When this cause is argued by such men as Christoph Bertram, Field Marshal Lord Carver, Admiral Noel Gayler, Professor Michael Howard, Henry Kissinger, François de Rose, Theo Sommer, and General Maxwell Taylor, to name only a few, it is fair to conclude that at least in its general direction the present argument is not outside the mainstream of thinking within the Alliance. Indeed there is evidence of renewed concern for conventional forces in governments too.

What should be added, in both public and private sectors, is a fresh, sustained, and careful consideration of the requirements and the benefits of deciding that the policy of the Atlantic Alliance should be to keep its nuclear weapons unused as long as others do the same. Our own belief, though we do not here assert it as proven, is that when this possibility is fully explored it will be evident that the advantages of the policy far outweigh its costs, and that this demonstration will help the peoples and governments of the Alliance to find the political will to move in this direction. In this spirit we go on to sketch the benefits that could come from such a change.

VII

The first possible advantage of a policy of no-first-use is in the management of the nuclear deterrent forces that would still be necessary. Once we escape from the need to plan for a first use that is credible, we can escape also from many of the complex arguments that have led to assertions that all sorts of new nuclear capabilities are necessary to create or restore a capability for something called "escalation dominance"—a capability to fight and "win" a nuclear war at any level. What would be needed, under no-first-use, is a set of capabilities we already have in overflowing measure—capabilities for appropriate retaliation to any kind of Soviet nuclear attack which would leave the Soviet Union in no doubt that it too should adhere to a policy of no-first-use. The Soviet government is already aware of the awful risk inherent in any use of these weapons, and there is no current or prospective Soviet "superiority" that would tempt anyone in Moscow toward nuclear adventurism. (All four of us are wholly unpersuaded by the argument advanced in recent years that the Soviet Union could ever rationally expect to gain from such a wild effort as a massive first strike on land-based American strategic missiles.)

Once it is clear that the only nuclear need of the Alliance is for adequately survivable and varied *second strike* forces, requirements for the modernization of major nuclear systems will become more modest than has been assumed. In particular we can escape from the notion that we must somehow match everything the rocket commanders in the Soviet Union extract from their government. It seems doubtful, also, that under such a policy it would be necessary or desirable to deploy neutron bombs. The savings permitted by more modest programs could go toward meeting the financial costs of our contribution to conventional forces.

It is important to avoid misunderstanding here. In the conditions of the 1980s, and in the absence of agreement on both sides to proceed to very large-scale reductions in nuclear forces, it is clear that large, varied, and survivable nuclear forces will still be necessary for nuclear deterrence. The point is not that we Americans should move unilaterally to some "minimum" force of a few tens or even hundreds of missiles, but rather that once we escape from the pressure to seem willing and able to use these weapons first, we shall find that our requirements are much less massive than is now widely supposed.

A posture of no-first-use should also go far to meet the understandable anxieties that underlie much of the new interest in nuclear disarmament, both in Europe and in our own country. Some of the proposals generated by this new interest may lack practicability for the present. For example, proposals to make "all" of Europe—from Portugal to Poland—a nuclear-free zone do not seem to take full account of the reality that thousands of long-range weapons deep in the Soviet Union will still be able to target Western Europe. But a policy of no-first-use, with its accompaniment of a reduced requirement for new Allied nuclear systems, should allow a considerable reduction in fears of all sorts. Certainly such a new policy would neutralize the highly disruptive argument currently put about in Europe: that plans for theater nuclear modernization reflect an American hope to fight a nuclear war limited to Europe. Such modernization might or might not be needed under a policy of no-first-use; that question, given the size and versatility of other existing and prospective American forces, would be a matter primarily for European decision (as it is today).

An effective policy of no-first-use will also reduce the risk of conventional aggression in Europe. That risk has never been as great as prophets of doom have claimed and has always lain primarily in the possibility that Soviet leaders might think they could achieve some quick and limited gain that would be accepted because no defense or reply could be concerted. That temptation has been much reduced by the Allied conventional deployments achieved in the last 20 years, and it would be reduced still further by the additional shift in the balance of Allied effort that a no-first-use policy would both permit and require. The risk that an adventurist Soviet leader might take the terrible gamble of conventional aggression was greater in the past than it is today, and is greater today than it would be under no-first-use, backed up by an effective conventional defense.

VIII

We have been discussing a problem of military policy, but our interest is also political. The principal immediate danger in the current military posture of the Alliance is not that it will lead to large-scale war, conventional or nuclear. The balance of terror, and the caution of both sides, appear strong enough today to prevent such a catastrophe, at least in the absence of some deeply destabilizing political change which might lead to panic or adventurism on either side. But the present unbalanced reliance on nuclear weapons, if long continued, might produce exactly such political change. The events of the last year have shown that differing perceptions of the role of nuclear weapons can lead to destructive recriminations, and when these differences are compounded by understandable disagreements on other matters such as Poland and the Middle East, the possibilities for trouble among Allies are evident.

The political coherence of the Alliance, especially in times of stress, is at least as important as the military strength required to maintain credible deterrence. Indeed the political requirement has, if anything, an even higher priority. Soviet leaders would be most pleased to help the Alliance fall into total disarray, and would much prefer such a development to the inescapable uncertainties of open conflict. Conversely, if consensus is re-established on a military policy that the peoples and governments of the Alliance can believe in, both political will and deterrent credibility will be reinforced. Plenty of hard questions will remain, but both fear and mistrust will be reduced, and they are the most immediate enemies.

There remains one underlying reality which could not be removed by even the most explicit declaratory policy of no-first-use. Even if the nuclear powers of the Alliance should join, with the support of other Allies, in a policy of no-first-use, and even if that decision should lead to a common declaration of such policy by these powers and the Soviet Union, no one on either side could guarantee beyond all possible doubt that if conventional warfare broke out on a large scale there would in fact be no use of nuclear weapons. We could not make that assumption about the Soviet Union, and we must recognize that Soviet leaders could not make it about us. As long as the weapons themselves exist, the possibility of their use will remain.

But this inescapable reality does not undercut the value of a no-first-use policy. That value is first of all for the internal health of the Western Alliance itself. A posture of effective conventional balance and survivable second-strike nuclear strength is vastly better for our own peoples and governments, in a deep sense more civilized, than one that forces the serious contemplation of "limited" nuclear scenarios that are at once terrifying and implausible.

There is strong reason to believe that no-first-use can also help in our relations with the Soviet Union. The Soviet government has repeatedly offered to join the West in declaring such a policy, and while such declarations may have only limited reliability, it would be wrong to disregard the real value to both sides of a jointly declared adherence to this policy. To renounce the first use of nuclear weapons is to accept an enormous burden of responsibility for any later violation. The existence of such a clearly declared common pledge would increase the cost and risk of any sudden use of nuclear weapons by either side and correspondingly reduce the political force of spoken or unspoken threats of such use.

A posture and policy of no-first-use also could help to open the path toward serious reduction of nuclear armaments on both sides. The nuclear decades have shown how hard it is to get agreements that really do constrain these weapons, and no one can say with assurance that any one step can make a decisive difference. But just as a policy of no-first-use should reduce the pressures on our side for massive new nuclear forces, it should help to increase the international incentives for the Soviet Union to show some restraint of its own. It is important not to exaggerate here, and certainly Soviet policies on procurement are not merely delayed mirror-images of ours. Nonetheless there are connections between what is said and what is done even in the Soviet Union, and there are incentives for moderation, even there, that could be strengthened by a jointly declared policy of renouncing first use. At a minimum such a declaration would give both sides additional reason to seek for agreements that would prevent a vastly expensive and potentially destabilizing contest for some kind of strategic advantage in outer space.

Finally, and in sum, we think a policy of no-first-use, especially if shared with the Soviet Union, would bring new hope to everyone in every country whose life is shadowed by the hideous possibility of a third great twentieth-century conflict in Europe—conventional or nuclear. It seems timely and even urgent to begin the careful study of a policy that could help to sweep this threat clean off the board of international affairs.

IX

We recognize that we have only opened this large question, that we have exhausted no aspect of it, and that we may have omitted important elements. We know that NATO is much more than its four strongest military members; we know that a policy of no-first-use in the Alliance would at once raise questions about America's stance in Korea and indeed other parts of Asia. We have chosen deliberately to focus on the central front of our central alliance, believing that a right choice there can only help toward right choices elsewhere.

What we dare to hope for is the kind of new and widespread consideration of the policy we have outlined that helped us 15 years ago toward SALT I, 25 years ago toward the Limited Test Ban, and 35 years ago toward the Alliance itself. Such consideration can be made all the more earnest and hopeful by keeping in mind one simple and frequently neglected reality: there has been no first use of nuclear weapons since 1945, and no one in any country regrets that fact. The right way to maintain this record is to recognize that in the age of massive thermonuclear overkill it no longer makes sense—if it ever did—to hold these weapons for any other purpose than the prevention of their use.

Note

[1] McGeorge Bundy was Special Assistant to the President for National Security Affairs from 1961 to 1966 and President of the Ford Foundation from 1966 to mid-1979. He is currently Professor of History at New York University.

George F. Kennan is Professor Emeritus at the Institute for Advanced Study, Princeton. He was US Ambassador to the Soviet Union, 1952, and to Yugoslavia, 1961–63, and is the author of *Soviet–American Relations, 1917–20* (2 vols.); *Memoirs* (2 vols.) and other works.

Robert S. McNamara was Secretary of Defense from 1961 to 1968 and President of the World Bank from 1968 to mid-1981.

Gerard Smith was Chief of the US Delegation to the Strategic Arms Limitations Talks (SALT) from 1969 to 1972, and is the author of *Doubletalk: The Story of SALT I.* He also served as Special Assistant to the Secretary of State for atomic energy affairs (1954–57), Director of the Policy Planning Staff of the Department of State (1957–61), a full-time consultant on the Multilateral Force (1961–64), and Ambassador at Large and Special Presidential Representative for non-proliferation matters (1977–80).

Nuclear weapons and the preservation of peace

Karl Kaiser, Georg Leber, Alois Mertes and Franz-Josef Schulze[1]

Reprinted by permission of Foreign Affairs, Summer 1982. Copyright 1982 by the Council on Foreign Relations, Inc.

A response to an American proposal for renouncing the first use of nuclear weapons

The appropriate strategy for the use of nuclear weapons has been the subject of discussion since the North Atlantic Alliance was founded. Open debate on these problems is part of the natural foundations of an Alliance consisting of democracies which relate to each other as sovereign partners. It is not the first time in the history of the Alliance that fears about the danger of nuclear war have caused concern and anxieties in all member countries, although these are more pronounced today than before. They must be taken seriously. The questions posed demand convincing answers, for in a democracy, policy on questions of peace and war requires constantly renewed legitimization.

When McGeorge Bundy, George F. Kennan, Robert S. McNamara and Gerard Smith submit a proposal to renounce the first use of nuclear weapons in Europe[2], the mere fact that it comes from respected American personalities with long years of experience in questions of security policy and the Alliance gives it particular weight. Their reflections must be taken particularly seriously in a country like the Federal Republic of Germany which has a special interest in preserving peace, because in case of war nuclear weapons could first be used on its territory.

All responsible people must face the issues of the discussion initiated by the four authors. It is necessary to think through all questions posed and not to select only those ideas which cater to widespread anxieties. What matters most is to concentrate not only on the prevention of nuclear war, but on how to prevent *any* war, conventional war as well. The decisive criterion in evaluating this proposal—like any new proposal—must be: Will it contribute to preserving, into the future, the peace and freedom of the last three decades?

Unfortunately, the current discussion on both sides of the Atlantic about the four authors' proposal has been rendered more difficult by a confusion between the option of the "first use" of nuclear weapons and the capability for a "first strike" with nuclear weapons. The authors themselves have unintentionally contributed to this confusion by using both terms. "First use" refers to the first use of a nuclear weapon regardless of its yield and place; even blowing up a bridge with a nuclear weapon in one's own territory would represent a first use. "First strike" refers to a preemptive disarming nuclear strike aimed at eliminating as completely as possible the entire strategic potential of the adversary. A first strike by the Alliance is not a relevant issue; such a strike must remain unthinkable in the future as it is now and has been in the past. The matter for debate should be exclusively the defensive first use of nuclear weapons by the Western Alliance.

II

The current NATO strategy of flexible response is intended to discourage an adversary from using or threatening the use of military force by confronting him with a full spectrum of deterrence and hence with an uncalculable risk. The strategy also aims at improving the tools of crisis management as a means of preventing conflict. The deterrent effect of the doctrine rests on three pillars:
— the political determination of all Alliance members to resist jointly any form of aggression or blackmail;
— the capability of the Alliance to react effectively at every level of aggression; and
— the flexibility to choose between different possible reactions—conventional or nuclear.
The primary goal of this strategy is the prevention of war. To this end it harnesses the revolutionary new and inescapable phenomenon of the nuclear age for its own purposes. Our era has brought humanity not only the curse of the unprecedented destructive power of nuclear weapons but also its twin, the dread of unleashing that power, grounded in the fear of self-destruction. Wherever nuclear weapons are present, war loses its earlier function as a continuation of politics by other means. Even more, the destructive power of these weapons has forced political leaders, especially those of nuclear weapons states, to weigh risks to a degree unknown in history.

The longest period of peace in European history is inconceivable without the war-preventing effect of nuclear weapons. During the same time span more than a hundred wars have taken place in Asia, Africa, and Latin America, where the numbers of dead, wounded and refugees run into the millions.

The continuous increase in the number of nuclear weapons—now comprising many thousands of warheads with ever more refined delivery systems—instills in many people, for understandable reasons, anxieties about the consequences of a war with a destructive power that exceeds the human imagination. But the only new factor here is that more people realize these consequences than in the past. Many political and military leaders were already aware of them when these weapons were developed and the first test results were presented. The fear of the consequences of such a war has to this day fortunately led to a policy which has made an essential contribution to preventing war in Europe—but which at the same time has regrettably stimulated the buildup of arsenals, since neither side wanted to lapse into a position of inferiority.

The strategy of flexible response attempts to counter any attack by the adversary—no matter what the level—in such a way that the aggressor can have no hope of advantage or success by triggering a military conflict, be it conventional or nuclear. The tight and indissoluble coupling of conventional forces and nuclear weapons on the European continent with the strategic potential of the United States confronts the Soviet Union with the incalculable risk that any military conflict between the two Alliances could escalate to a nuclear war. The primary function of nuclear weapons is deterrence in order to prevent aggression and blackmail.

The coupling of conventional and nuclear weapons has rendered war between East and West unwageable and unwinnable up to now. It is the inescapable paradox of this strategy of war prevention that the will to conduct nuclear war must be demonstrated in order to prevent war at all. Yet the ensuing indispensable presence of nuclear weapons and the constantly recalled visions of their possible destructive effect, should they ever be used in a war, make many people anxious.

The case is similar with regard to the limitation of nuclear war: the strategy of massive retaliation was revised because, given the growing potential of destruction, the threat of responding even to low levels of aggression with a massive use of nuclear weapons became increasingly incredible. A threat once rendered incredible would no longer have been able to prevent war in Europe. Thus, in the mid-1960s the Europeans supported the introduction of flexible response, which made the restricted use of nuclear weapons—but also the limitation of any such use—an indispensable part of deterrence aimed at preventing even "small" wars in Europe. Critics of nuclear deterrence today misinterpret this shift in strategy, drawing from it a suspicion of conspiracy between the superpowers to wage a limited nuclear war on European territory and at the expense of the Europeans.

A renunciation of the first use of nuclear weapons would certainly rob the present strategy of war prevention—which is supported by the government and the opposition in the Federal Republic of Germany, as well as by a great majority of the population—of a decisive characteristic. One cannot help concluding that the Soviet Union would thereby be put in a position where it could, once again, calculate its risk and thus be able to wage war in Europe. It would no longer have to fear that nuclear weapons would inflict unacceptable damage to its own territory. We therefore fear that a credible renunciation of the first use of nuclear weapons would, once again, make war more probable.

A decisive weakness of the proposal by the four authors lies in their assertion that a no-first-use policy would render wars less likely, without producing sufficient evidence. Even though the restoration of the conventional balance which they call for (and which will be examined below) increases the conventional risk for the Soviet assault formations, such a policy would liberate the Soviet Union from the decisive nuclear risk—and thereby from the constraint that has kept the Soviet Union, up to now, from using military force, even for limited purposes, against Western Europe. The liberation from nuclear risk would, of course, benefit the United States to the same degree. It must be questioned, there-

45

fore, whether renunciation of first use represents a contribution to the "internal health of the Western Alliance itself" (page 39) or whether, instead, a no-first-use policy increases insecurity and fear of ever more probable war.

The argumentation of the four American authors is considerably weakened by their tendency to think in worst-case scenarios. They assume almost fatalistically a total irrationality of state behavior and the impossibility of controlling a supposedly irreversible escalation. We share the authors' opinion that the kind of Soviet adventurism that would undertake a nuclear first strike against the United States can be excluded as a serious possibility. We are also familiar with the recent studies which assert that a limited nuclear war probably becomes more and more difficult to control with increasing escalation. Here we cannot disagree. However, one must at the same time ask under what circumstances a first use of Western nuclear weapons in Europe—should it happen at all—would be probable. This is only thinkable in a situation where a large-scale conventional attack by the Warsaw Pact could no longer be countered by conventional means alone, thus forcing NATO to a limited use of nuclear weapons: small weapons in small quantities, perhaps even only a warning shot. All indications suggest that both sides would be extremely cautious, in order to avoid precisely the dreaded, possibly uncontrollable escalation which some studies rightfully present as a danger, and which the advocates of a no-first-use policy present as a certainty.

III

The Western Alliance is an alliance of equals. Its cohesion is therefore based on the greatest possible realization of the principles of equal risks, equal burdens and equal security. The present NATO strategy reflects this principle. It guarantees that the American military potential with all its components, conventional and nuclear, is included in the defense of Europe. Not only the inhabitants of the Federal Republic of Germany but also American citizens help bear the risks, the conventional as well as the nuclear. The indivisibility of the security of the Alliance as a whole and of its territory creates the credibility of deterrence.

The conclusions that can be drawn from the four authors' recommendations with regard to the commitment of the United States to the defense of Europe are profoundly disturbing. To be sure, they assert that no-first-use does not represent an abandonment of the American protective guarantee for Western Europe, but "only its redefinition" (page 33). Indeed, that would be the case, but in the form of a withdrawal from present commitments of the United States.

The opinion of the four American authors that "the one clearly definable firebreak against the worldwide disaster of general nuclear war is the one that stands between all other kinds of conflict and any use whatsoever of nuclear weapons" (page 32), amounts to no less than limiting the existing nuclear guarantee of protection by the United States for their non-nuclear Alliance partners to the case of prior use of nuclear weapons by the Soviet Union. Even in the case of a large-scale conventional attack against the entire European NATO territory, the Soviet Union could be certain that its own land would remain a sanctuary as long as it did not itself resort to nuclear weapons. This would apply even more to surprise operations aimed at the quick occupation of parts of Western Europe which are hardly defensible by conventional means.

In such a case, those attacked would have to bear the destruction and devastation of war alone. It is only too understandable that for years the Soviet Union has, therefore, pressed for a joint American–Soviet renunciation of first use of nuclear weapons, on occasion in the guise of global proposals. If the ideas of the authors were to be followed, conventional conflicts in Europe would no longer involve any existential risk for the territory of the Soviet Union and—despite the increased American participation in the conventional defense of Europe suggested by the authors—would be without such risk for the territory of the United States as well.

The authors' suggestion that "even the most responsible choice of even the most limited nuclear actions to prevent even the most imminent conventional disaster should be left out of authorized policy" (page 36) makes completely clear that a withdrawal of the United States from its previous guarantee is at stake. They thus advise Western Europe to capitulate should defeat threaten, for example if the Federal Republic were in danger of being overrun conventionally. The American nuclear guarantee would be withdrawn.

The authors assert that the implementation of their astonishing proposal would not be taken in Europe, and especially in the Federal Republic, "as evidence of a reduced American interest in the Alliance and in effective overall deterrence" (page 35), but that, on the contrary, it would be the best means "for keeping the Alliance united and effective" (page 35). On this point we beg to differ: the proposed no-first-use policy would destroy the confidence of Europeans and especially of Germans in the European–American Alliance as a community of risk, and would endanger the strategic unity of the Alliance and the security of Western Europe.

IV

Given a renunciation of nuclear first use, the risks of a potential aggressor doubtlessly become more calculable. Moreover, the significance of Soviet conventional superiority would thereby increase dramatically. Conventional war in Europe would once again become possible. It could again become a continuation of politics by other means. Moreover, NATO would face a fundamentally different conventional threat. The elimination of the nuclear risk would free the Warsaw Pact from the necessity to disperse attack forces. As a result NATO would have to produce significantly higher numbers of combat forces than today.

The assertion of the four American authors that there is a tendency to overestimate the conventional strength of the Soviet Union does not correspond to the most recent East–West force comparison undertaken by NATO. They do admit, however, that a no-first-use policy requires stronger conventional forces; in their opinion the Alliance is capable of accomplishing such a buildup within realistic budgets. We believe the authors considerably underestimate the political and financial difficulties which stand in the way of establishing a conventional balance through increased armament by the West. The case would be different if through negotiations a conventional balance could be reached by reductions in Warsaw Pact forces. The authors do not explore this possibility, but the long years of as yet unsuccessful negotiations for mutual and balanced force reductions (MBFR) demonstrate the obstacles on this path.

The establishment of balance through the buildup of Western conventional forces would likewise be extremely difficult. The costs would be of a magnitude that would dramatically exceed the framework of present defense budgets. Suggestions by the authors about possible savings in the nuclear area in case of no-first-use are of little benefit for the non-nuclear weapons states of Europe. (Such savings, incidentally, imply a significant reduction of the Western nuclear arsenal.) In our judgment, the United States and Great Britain would have to introduce the draft, and the European countries would have to extend their period of military service. Because of the necessity for a significantly higher number of military forces, the Federal Republic of Germany would have to accept on its territory large contingents of additional troops, those of the allies and its own: the Federal Republic would be transformed into a large military camp for an indefinite period. Do the four American authors seriously believe that the preconditions for the buildup required by their proposal exist in Western Europe—and the United States?

Even if an approximate conventional balance could be achieved in Europe, two disadvantages to the detriment of Western Europe would remain: first, the Soviet Union has a geographic advantage, it can always quickly change the balance of forces from the relative proximity of its territory; second, there would always be the possibility, not even excluded by the American authors, that, despite no-first-use, conventional war could in an advanced phase degenerate into nuclear war.

Moreover, in commenting skeptically about the idea of a nuclear-free zone, the authors themselves point out that the Soviet Union can move nuclear weapons relatively quickly from deep within its territory into such a zone. If a no-first-use policy is linked with a complete or at least substantial withdrawal of tactical nuclear weapons—and that is apparently meant by the authors—it would, moreover, be easier for the Soviet Union to reach Central Europe with nuclear weapons from its own territory than for the United States.

For Germans and other Europeans whose memory of the catastrophe of conventional war is still alive and on whose densely populated territory both pacts would confront each other with the destructive power of modern armies, the thought of an ever more probable conventional war is terrifying.

To Germans and other Europeans, an ever more probable conventional war is, therefore, no alternative to war prevention through the current strategy, including the option of a first use of nuclear weapons. While the four authors link their proposal with the laudable intention of reducing European anxieties about nuclear war, its implementation could result in anxieties about a more probable conventional war soon replacing anxieties about the much less probable nuclear war. The anti-nuclear protest movement in Europe suspects the United States and the Soviet Union of intending to wage a limited nuclear war on the territory, and at the expense, of the Europeans. Were the movement to apply the logic of its argument to the case of no-first-use, it would naturally arrive at a new suspicion: that a conventional war could now also be waged on European territory and at European expense—particularly since a nuclear risk for the superpowers would no longer exist. All that would then be necessary would be to paint a vivid picture of the terrors of conventional war—once again thinkable—and the insecurity of the Europeans would receive new and dangerous reinforcement.

V

We are grateful for the manner in which the four American authors of a no-first-use proposal have evaluated the particularly exposed position of the Federal Republic of Germany and the special difficulties which ensue for its security policy. It is, however, striking that they do not deal at all with a problem which does not, to be sure, pose itself for a world power like the United States but which the Federal Republic of Germany and all European Alliance partners have to keep in mind: the problem of protecting themselves from political pressure and preserving their free society.

The protection of a free society based on the rule of law is just as important a part of a policy of preserving peace as the prevention of war. War can always be avoided at the price of submission. It is naturally more obvious to Europeans, and in particular to Germans—in their precarious position within a divided country—than to the population of the American superpower that an actual military superiority of the Soviet Union, or a feeling of inferiority in Western Europe, can be exploited to put political pressure on Western Europe.

The feeling of vulnerability to political blackmail, as a result of the constant demonstration of superior military might, would be bound to grow considerably if the nuclear protector of the Atlantic Alliance were to declare—as suggested by the four authors—that it would not use nuclear weapons in case of a conventional attack against Europe. This applies in particular to those exposed areas which even with considerable improvements of conventional forces can only with great difficulty be conventionally defended, or not at all: these include, for example, North Norway, Thrace, and in particular, West Berlin. The protection of these areas lies solely in the incalculability of the American reaction.

The advice of the authors to renounce the use of nuclear weapons even in the face of pending conventional defeat of Western Europe is tantamount to suggesting that "rather Red than dead" would be the only remaining option for those Europeans then still alive. Were such advice to become policy, it would destroy the psychological basis necessary for the will to self-defense. Such counsel would strengthen tendencies in Europe to seek gradual voluntary and timely salvation in preventive "good conduct" and growing subservience vis-à-vis the Soviet Union for fear of war and Soviet superiority. The result would be to restrict the very freedom that the Alliance was founded to protect.

VI

The four American authors advance a number of skeptical arguments about the NATO two-track decision of December 1979 which amount to a rejection of this decision. They attack one alleged motive for the double-track decision, the desire for balance below the intercontinental level of nuclear weapons. Although the notion of balance did occasionally appear in public discussion by politicians who advanced it to legitimize the NATO decision in view of the growing Soviet medium-range nuclear potential, balance was not a leitmotiv and did not play an essential role in shaping the decision itself. Were that the case, the potential of the Western nuclear weapons envisaged (should negotiations fail) would have had to be significantly larger than the planned 572 systems, which—together with the already existing Western weapons—amount to only a fraction of comparable Soviet systems. From the very beginning, the double-track decision was essentially conceived to couple the intercontinental with the Europe-related nuclear weapons force.

We share the concern which the four authors express about the potentially negative impact which the controversies on the NATO double-track decision could have on the Alliance. However, unlike them, we do not conclude that NATO should forego the double-track decision. Our conclusion is based on three arguments in particular:

First, the Soviet Union must recognize that it would also be to its own advantage to abandon its absolute notion of security—for such a notion condemns any attempt at stabilizing the East–West relationship to failure. The Soviet decision to develop, produce and deploy the SS-20 missile in Eastern Europe was made during the first half of the 1970s, i.e., during the period in which the West actively pursued genuine détente. It must have been clear to every Soviet planner that, given the quality of this weapons system, located below the strategic level (which was moving toward parity and accordingly codified in SALT), its expansion would dislocate the nuclear deterrence system by regionalizing the threat.

Messages from Western and German sources directed with great urgency at the Soviet Union during the 1970s—among them a meeting between Federal Chancellor Helmut Schmidt and General Secretary Leonid Brezhnev in May 1978—were simply ignored. The buildup of this rocket arsenal continued relentlessly and still does. In addition, new modern systems of shorter and medium reach were developed; they are now in production and deployment. All of these add a new quantitative and qualitative dimension to Soviet armament.

These developments raise the depressing question of whether and how the dynamics of Soviet armament policy can be influenced at all. In any case, in the interests of security and peace, such attempts must not be abandoned. Only an announcement and demonstration of the capacity to implement a Western medium-range armament program (572 Pershing II and cruise missiles) which would result in a loss of military and political options for the Soviets could, if at all, induce the Soviet leadership to halt and reduce its armament.

Second, where would such a development end if, by renouncing the implementation of the double-track decision, the Alliance were to let the Soviet medium- and short-range nuclear potential grow to thousands of systems without an adequate counterweight on the Western side and with continued strategic parity?

Two consequences would emerge: in the first place, the American nuclear guarantee for Europe would lose its credibility. The view, also shared by the four authors, that the Soviet medium-range potential can be dealt with by American systems assigned to NATO (which are, by the way, counted in SALT and not well usable for tactical functions) lacks conclusiveness. As such a striking Soviet superiority increasingly develops, the United States loses the capability for escalation and thereby its credibility. This has a destabilizing effect.

In the second place, we are concerned by the possibility that with an acceptance of further growth of Soviet nuclear superiority below the intercontinental level, a potential for threat emerges which can be used for political pressures. In this case, the well-meant advice that only those can be blackmailed who let themselves be is of little use, since these weapons are assumed to be unusable because of the risk involved. In 1956 Khrushchev threatened Paris and London with nuclear weapons. At that time his threats had little impact under conditions of American strategic superiority. Imagine what a repetition of such threats would be like under conditions of striking Soviet superiority in the field of medium-range weapons and of the anxieties of the West European public caused by the nuclear debate. Under these circumstances politicians in the Western democracies would be put under a degree of pressure unimaginable in the 1950s.

Third, the long-term impact of a failure of the double-track decision is a cause of concern to us. The anti-nuclear protest, in our opinion, will not disappear but will in all probability remain a permanent characteristic of the political situation in Western Europe for years. This protest and the legitimate concerns which it expresses must be taken very seriously, but at the same time it should not be overlooked that it represents a minority—which, however, enjoys powerful support from the media on both sides of the Atlantic. Security policy, like any other policy in democracies, is determined by majorities and must be accepted by minorities. If, in the case of the double-track decision, the existing clear majority should fail to prevail in the face of a minority in fundamental opposition to it—and one likely to persist in the future—much more would be at stake than the decision in question. This has been recognized by parts of the protest movement—and in Moscow as well. The capability of democratic majorities to define and implement security policy in the future is also at stake in the double-track decision.

VII

Special emphasis on the renunciation of *one* form of force—the first use of nuclear weapons—decreases the importance of the general prohibition against the use of force laid down in Article 2 of the U.N. Charter, resulting for all

51

practical purposes in a diminution of the prohibition against the use of conventional force. The Federal Republic of Germany has always adhered to the principle of the general renunciation of the use of force. It reconfirmed this commitment when entering NATO, as well as in the Eastern Treaties of the early 1970s and the Final Act of Helsinki in 1975. The Federal Republic shares with other Alliance partners the view that it is legally questionable and politically harmful to separate the question of specific arms from the general renunciation of the use of force.

Government and opposition within the Federal Republic are in complete agreement on this issue. Indeed the question must be posed whether, with a prohibition of the first use of nuclear weapons, the first use of other weapons becomes less prohibited and whether a country threatened by a conventionally highly armed neighbor will then be less protected by the prohibition of the use of force.

To an essential degree the anti-nuclear protest in Europe derives from the rejection of nuclear arms procurement up to barely imaginable potentials of destruction, from the waste of resources which it engenders in a world of poverty, and from the possibility of war under nuclear conditions. We consider these concerns legitimate, although we do not share essential conclusions of the movement. In view of the burdens of defense policy in the nuclear age which the citizens in our democracies have to bear, it is the constant duty of government and opposition to exploit all available possibilities to decrease tensions and potentials for destruction by means of cooperation, confidence-building measures, arms control and disarmament.

Unlike the four American authors, we do not consider a renunciation of the option of a first use as the answer to the existing concerns and anxieties over nuclear weapons. Instead, we see the answer in a creative and realistic policy of arms control and disarmament. We consider the NATO double-track decision of December 1979, combining arms control negotiations and the announcement of armaments in case of failure, as an innovative step. We welcome the beginning of negotiations on medium-range weapons in Geneva and the "zero option" proposed by President Reagan. The reduction of excessive Soviet armament is the main goal of this proposal; in a way comprehensible to everybody, it now places on the Soviet Union the responsibility for potential armament measures of the West. We welcome, furthermore, the readiness announced by both world powers to open negotiations on strategic weapons, as well as the proposals on START presented by President Reagan at Eureka on May 9. The NATO ministerial meeting of May 1981 and the declaration of the NATO summit in Bonn of June 1982 unequivocally express the continuity of the basic philosophy of the Alliance, which seeks security only through a combination of adequate defense capacity and a policy of cooperation and negotiations to eliminate the causes of tensions.

The four American authors hope that a policy of no-first-use could help to clear the way towards a serious reduction of nuclear weapons on both sides. Their further comments on this topic, however, suggest that they themselves do not entertain exaggerated hopes. Indeed, the experience of recent years in the field of tactical nuclear weapons gives little cause for hope that the Soviet side is ready for genuine reductions. Moreover, it is questionable whether the Soviets are ready to renounce their conventional superiority built up at great sacrifice, stubbornly defended during decades and energetically expanded in recent years, at the very moment when such a superiority would be given an increased and decisive importance by a NATO renunciation of first use of nuclear weapons.

We share many of the concerns about the risks of nuclear war. They lead us to conclude that an energetic attempt to reduce the *dependence on an early first use* of nuclear weapons must be undertaken. To be sure, the authors also mention a "no-early-first-use" policy (page 36) as a possible alternative, but in the last analysis they discard it as a mere variation of nuclear options and therefore call for a clear decision in favor of a renunciation of "any first use of nuclear weapons" (page 36).

A reduction of dependence on an early use of nuclear weapons should, in the first place, be attempted through mutual, balanced and verifiable reductions of conventional forces by means of East–West negotiations which result in an adequate conventional balance. We have pointed out how difficult it would be to restore such a balance by the buildup of Western conventional armament. In our opinion the essential precondition posed by the authors for their suggested renunciation of first use can, therefore, not be fulfilled.

In sum, we consider efforts to raise the nuclear threshold by a strengthening of conventional options to be urgently necessary. The reduction of the dependence on first use, in particular on early first use of nuclear weapons, should be a question of high political priority in our countries.

The Western Alliance has committed itself to a renunciation from the very beginning: the renunciation of the first use of *any* force. The entire military planning, structure and deployment of forces are geared exclusively toward defense. The presence of nuclear weapons has contributed essentially to the success of the Alliance in preventing war and preserving freedom for three decades. We are convinced that a reduction of the dependence on an early use of nuclear weapons would serve this purpose. Under the circumstances of the foreseeable future, however, a renunciation of the option of first use would be contrary to the security interests of Europe and the entire Alliance.

Notes

[1] Karl Kaiser is Director of the Research Institute of the German Society for Foreign Affairs in Bonn.

Georg Leber is a Social Democrat member and Vice-President of the West German Bundestag; a former trade union chairman, from 1972 to 1978 he was Defence Minister of the Federal Republic.

Alois Mertes is a Christian Democrat member of the Bundestag, a member of its Foreign Affairs Committee, and foreign policy spokesman of the CDU/CSU parliamentary Party; he is a former member of the foreign service.

General Franz-Josef Schulze (ret.) was Commander in Chief of Allied Forces Central Europe from 1977 to 1979 and Deputy Chief of Staff, Allied Command Europe, from 1973 to 1976.

The German text of this article was published in *Europa-Archiv*.

[2] Reproduced in the present volume, pages 29–41.

Part III
Discussion papers

Paper 1.   The necessity, preconditions and consequences of a no-first-use policy

Horst Afheldt

Research Fellow in alternative defence, Max-Planck-Institut für Sozialwissenschaften, Starnberg, FR Germany

I. The necessity for a no-first-use policy

Apart from all the well-founded moral arguments against the first use of nuclear weapons, there are powerful political arguments as well. These are as follows:

1. Defending Europe with nuclear weapons would destroy the territory being defended. Why?

The military objective of defence with nuclear weapons is to repel the attacker. Either this defence succeeds and destroys the enemy's tank force or it fails. If it fails, the battle is lost. Success therefore requires the use of an adequate number of nuclear weapons to ensure the destruction of the enemy's forces. The basic laws of warfare will make it impossible for both sides to limit nuclear war to the use of a few nuclear weapons only. Clausewitz's rules are relevant here, summed up by Guderian as follows: Don't whistle with the fingers, smash with the fist! What such a use of nuclear weapons would mean for the population of the Federal Republic of Germany, for example, is shown in figure 1.1. The bottom axis gives the number of warheads exploding on the territory of the Federal Republic of Germany. The graph shows the numbers killed and wounded. The upper two curves illustrate the effects of ground explosions, with cities as targets. The lower two curves assume that the power using nuclear weapons—the WTO or NATO—tries to avoid collateral damage and therefore does not attack cities. For example 1 000 Hiroshima type bombs would produce more than 10 million casualties, even if an attempt were made to avoid cities. But there are more than 10 000 nuclear weapons stationed on, or targeted on, European soil today.

2. What about *deterrence* by nuclear weapons?

Here we have to distinguish between deterrence of a conventional attack by the threat to respond with a *first use* of nuclear weapons, and the deterrence of an attack with nuclear weapons by the threat of *retaliation in kind*.

Figure 1.1. Defending Europe with nuclear weapons—probable effects on FR Germany

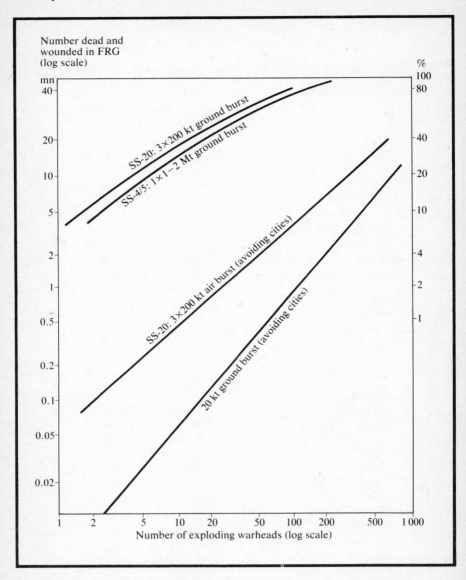

Source: von Weizäcker (ed.), *Kriegsfolgen und Kriegsverhütung* (Munich, 1970), p. 28. Calculations by Philipp Sonntag.

It is generally accepted that a second-strike deterrence of a first use by the enemy is credible, so long as there is a well-protected second-strike capability.

However, the aim of deterring a nuclear attack by the threat of retaliation is not in fact served by NATO's tactical nuclear weapons, nor by the Pershing II or cruise missiles. The reason is that all these systems are not well-protected: they are vulnerable to a Soviet first strike.

3. Can a Soviet conventional attack on Europe be deterred by NATO's threat to use nuclear weapons first? Such a threat is no longer credible—to quote Henry Kissinger: "The principal evasion was the refusal to face the fact that strategic nuclear weapons could continue to counter-balance local Soviet advantages only if the US strategic arsenal was clearly superior to that of the Soviet Union—superiority being defined as the ability to destroy the opposing nuclear capability at acceptable cost".[1]

On this reasoning the only way to make NATO's first use of nuclear weapons credible would be for the United States to re-establish a massive superiority in its strategic arsenal. However, if it were successful in doing this, it might well have a first-strike capability which it could be tempted to use; equally, the Soviet Union might be tempted to try a pre-emptive first strike in the hope of saving at least some of its nuclear weapon assets. The risk of war would be increased.

It is certainly true that there is some deterrence value in nuclear weapons: the fear that a conventional attack might provoke a nuclear war has some effect. But a policy which uses nuclear weapons for deterrence in this way has to be absolutely fail safe if a great catastrophe is to be avoided. It requires absolute confidence that in all future crises all governments concerned—US, Soviet, German, British or French—avoid any mistaken decisions. The historical record strongly suggests that such confidence would be misplaced.

II. Is there a way out?

There could be wide agreement over the proposition that NATO should not depend on the first use of nuclear weapons. The question is—how should it set about eliminating this dependence?

The most common answer—and one which has been given since the 1960s—has been that NATO should strengthen its conventional forces adequately. Why has this not been done?

The simple explanation is this. When NATO set about strengthening its conventional forces, the WTO did the same. Thus, the WTO retained its numerical superiority, at a higher level of armaments. So long as the existing structure of NATO conventional forces is retained, there is not much chance that the Soviet Union would allow NATO to improve its relative position.

There are two main reasons. First, both sides use 'worst case' analysis: they want security in the worst case. For example, on the Soviet side, the Soviet Union will take into account the 'worst case' with Polish, Hungarian and East German troops proving to be of doubtful military value. With both sides using worst case analysis, there is little prospect of reaching an agreement on parity.

The second reason arises from the military structure of the armies on both sides. All these armies in Europe are the children of Hitler's tank armies, designed for attack and *Blitzkrieg* in World War II. The historical facts of the 1940s forced both the Red Army and the US expeditionary force to prepare for attack, since in 1942 Europe was occupied by the Third Reich and had to be liberated. The army structure has not changed, in principle, since then. Each weapon system has been modernized, with new tanks replacing old ones, and becoming two to three times more expensive: but there has been no change in conventional force structure. The great shortcoming of this structure is that it gives the decisive advantage to the attacking side—which is not surprising, since it was for this purpose that the structure was developed. This structure, with armies on both sides prepared for offensive operations, is in itself destabilizing. It would become even more destabilizing if NATO were to build up its capacity further for pushing an attack deep into WTO territory.

Moreover, if NATO were to establish conventional forces with the same capability of conducting offensive operations as those of the WTO, this could lead to another disastrous consequence: the first use of nuclear weapons by the Soviet Union. As General Gallois has pointed out, it is only a question of time before the Soviet Union will have a low yield missile as accurate as the Pershing II. With such missiles the Soviet Union could destroy the whole structure of NATO's conventional forces in a first strike, without destroying Europe completely, since NATO's conventional defence relies on a limited number of highly vulnerable targets, such as airfields and communication centres. After such a first strike, NATO would have the choice of either capitulating or retaliating with nuclear weapons: if it chose the latter course, this would destroy Europe completely. Retaliation in such a case, is therefore, not very probable—and consequently the deterrence value of the threat of retaliation is very low.

The danger of a Soviet first strike would become even greater if NATO sought to improve its conventional defence according to the plan currently put forward by General Rogers. This plan calls for the use of conventional weapons for deep interdiction against both fixed and mobile targets in the territory of WTO countries. This strategy—both for its information and its guidance systems—is heavily dependent on radio communication systems. Yet these systems could be totally disrupted by a very limited first use of nuclear weapons by WTO countries if they were to explode an appropriate nuclear weapon at an appropriate altitude, in such a way as to induce an electro-magnetic pulse. A first use of a nuclear weapon of this kind would, in those circumstances, have a very high military pay-off, and consequently would be very attractive.

Inappropriate improvements of conventional defence, therefore, may even lead to a drastic lowering of the nuclear threshold. To avoid this trap, NATO might try to deter the Soviet Union from using their nuclear weapons. But if NATO presents the Soviet Union with important military targets for nuclear weapons, it is extremely attractive from the military point of view for the Soviet Union to attack these targets. Yet it is only the difference between threat and attraction which counts for deterrence. Therefore NATO has to threaten on an extremely high level to overcome the very strong attraction of the important military targets which NATO offers. There is no way of knowing in advance whether that deterrence will be effective. So that policy contains the risk of self-destruction.

A more reliable form of deterrence is to *reduce* the Soviet Union's *military interest* in using nuclear weapons, by not presenting important military targets. That means changing the whole structure of conventional defence, which does indeed lead to a promising way out of the dilemma. The key propositions are:

1. To avoid a structure which offers important targets for WTO nuclear weapons.
2. To change the conventional structure, from one developed 40 years ago for attack, to one which is especially designed for defence in Europe.

The no-target principle is fundamental. If strictly applied, it would lead to a network of small, well-hidden units all over the country. Deployment of this kind not only denies the attacking forces important tactical targets, it also refuses them their strategic aim. This aim of a tank attack is a 'blitzkrieg' type breakthrough: if there is no line to break through, this strategy fails.

A second important principle is that of specialization. The military structure must specialize on defence, because that is what is wanted in Europe. Since west Europeans do not want to attack, and are not interested in a first strike, there is no need to be prepared to do these things.

If arms control is wanted—and that surely is the case—then there is a third principle, which could be described as the categorical imperative of the nuclear age. It is to make only those military preparations which, if they were made on the enemy's side, could be accepted as not increasing their military threat; and only those military preparations which make it impossible for either side to exploit military power for political purposes.

This principle obviously excludes any first-strike policy; it also excludes any buildup of conventional tank armies on either side.

With specialization on defence, peace becomes more stable if one side copies the other side's defence preparations. Even if it does not, specialized effective defence preparations remove an enemy's option for attack: so the change to a specialized defence policy can be unilateral.

How can those principles be implemented in European defence?

The Study Group on Alternative Security Policies at the Max-Planck-Institut in Starnberg[2] has developed a model of defence which follows these three principles. This new defence structure is based on three pillars.

The *first pillar* is a pioneer-infantry network of small units, dispersed all over the country. On average there would be 3–4 men for each square kilometre. They would always be stationed in the same territory, they would know that territory thoroughly and would therefore be able to prepare that territory for defence in an optimal way. They would have to be equipped with anti-personnel weapons, with mines, and with cheap short-range missile launchers to shoot mines into an attacking tank column. But first of all they would have to be equipped with sophisticated anti-tank weapons. All these weapons follow the principle of not providing a target.

In a defensive network troops would dig themselves in, and so would not offer targets. They would hide the anti-tank weapons at a distance of 200–300 metres, in places where those weapons would have a good chance of destroying attacking tank forces. Then the soldiers, protected in their dugouts, teleguide their weapons systems. The same system would be used for anti-personnel weapons, for example machine guns. So the no-target principle can be used in the deployment of these weapons.

To develop such weapons for defensive networks, the components of the existing weapon systems would have to be taken and put together in a new way, one appropriate for a defensive network. The efficiency of an infantry network of this kind has been studied by the West German Army, and although the studies were conducted by persons not sympathetic to the whole concept, in general they suggest that this infantry network would be highly efficient.

The main argument against it is that the enemy might concentrate a very heavy attack. The critics are convinced that the enemy could force its way through the network in this way. Is that objection well-founded? It might be so if it were not for the *second pillar* of this structure—the precision-guided artillery rocket network.

Figure 1.2. The influence of precision: an attack on a 50 km front with 10 000 tanks

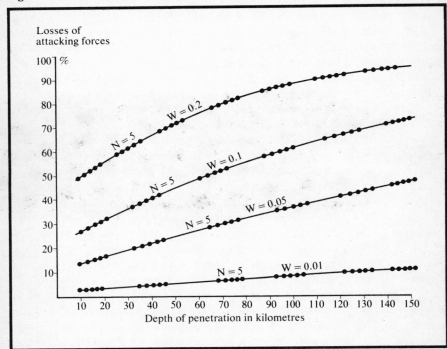

Source: Afheldt, H., *Defensive Verteidigung*, p. 117, Figure ARI5b.

Notes: N = number of missiles per square kilometre: W = kill probability.

The US Army has just ordered 400 000 artillery rockets for 10 billion D-Marks. That is equivalent to the cost of 100 fighter aircraft. These rockets have a range of 40–50 kilometres. Suppose there are five of these 40-kilometre-range precision-guided missiles for each square kilometre. Figure 1.2 shows what would happen in the case of an attack by 10 000 armoured vehicles on a 50 kilometre front. If we assume that each missile has a single-shot kill probability (W) of only 20 per cent against one enemy target ($W = 0.2$), then, after a penetration of 10 kilometres on a 50 kilometre front, the enemy would have lost 50 per cent of its tanks. Even if the missiles have a single-shot kill probability of only 10 per cent ($W = 0.1$), then the enemy would have lost 50 per cent of its forces after penetrating 65 kilometres.

It is true that the 400 000 missiles ordered currently by the United States Army probably do not have a high single-shot kill probability. But new missiles with terminal-guided systems are expected soon. The most important parameters are the range of the rockets and the kill probability; these parameters are interrelated.

The ideal rocket for this purpose is one fired vertically from an extremely cheap tube. The expensive guiding system is put in the missile itself. If it is the launcher which is expensive, then an attempt will be made to use it several times. But once it has been used the launcher will be targeted by the enemy's artillery; and—following our general principle—targets must be avoided. So the ideal rocket is a rocket which is fired vertically from a single one-way tube and guided by the guidance system *in* the missile.

A rocket which can fly 40–80 kilometres and hit a target with a high probability is, of course, a very effective weapon. But who knows where the target is? Today this information problem is really very difficult. Information is obtained by air surveillance, by teleguided cruise missiles and so on. All these methods are complicated and very expensive. But when there is an infantry network, the whole territory is covered by small units. Wherever the enemy appears in that network, his position becomes evident. These units can then direct the artillery missiles against the enemy. And for this they have to be linked with the artillery rocket system by the *third pillar*, the information network.

This information network has to ensure communications between the local infantry units themselves, between these infantry units and the precision-guided artillery missile network, and between both networks and the high command.

This triad of networks is much more effective than the defence structure of today. Some reasons for this higher efficiency are set out in table 1.1.

The idea of abandoning a first-use policy is, of course, not simply (or indeed mainly) an idea emanating from the peace movements. There are significant signs that the military establishments on both sides of the Atlantic are moving in that direction. However, their proposed restructuring of NATO's conventional defence is very different from that envisaged here. The approach recommended by the Supreme Allied Commander in Europe, General Rogers, is based on a far more complex and expensive assumption: that it is possible to cut off the second and third echelons of the WTO forces deep in the territories of those countries.[3] For purposes of this strategy, precision-guided conventional cruise missiles and

Table 1.1. Relative efficiency of the systems

Model for a defensive network	NATO system in 1982
90 per cent fighters, small logistics	10 per cent fighters, big logistics
Simple command and control	Complicated command and control
No target for enemy forces	Big targets for enemy forces
90 per cent chance of seeing the enemy first	50 per cent chance of seeing the enemy first
Quick reaction by missiles	Slow reaction by the movement of mechanized forces
Chance to avoid collateral damage high	Chance to avoid collateral damage low
No dependence on air superiority	Dependence on at least partial air superiority

conventional medium-range ballistic missiles would be needed.

There would, of course, be insoluble arms control problems if there were both nuclear and conventional medium-range weapons on German soil. The Soviet Union has two options against these conventional medium-range weapon systems. One option against cruise missiles is missile defence. It is true that it is not easy to develop missile defence against cruise missiles. But it is not impossible, especially with look-down shoot-down systems.

If the Soviet Union were seen to be developing defences of this kind, NATO would have to buy more and more cruise missiles, to buy new cruise missiles which are supersonic, to deploy anti-missile capabilities in the missiles, and so on. NATO would have to invest very substantial resources in maintaining a survivable cruise missile force, since this force would be the backbone of the new policy of non-reliance on nuclear weapons.

The Soviet Union could also build conventional medium-range missiles and cruise missiles itself. Such missiles would be very effective against NATO's current defence structure, which depends on large logistics, airfields, movements of columns of tanks, and so on. So NATO would also have to construct defences against Soviet cruise missiles; otherwise it would again become dependent on the first use of nuclear weapons. And against the medium-range ballistic missiles of the enemy, both sides have one option only: pre-emptive attack. So the conventional confrontations would be perpetuated and an extremely high crisis instability would occur.

This is because this new structure of deployment is suitable for both defence and attack: and both sides would apply their usual worst case analysis to the new military picture.

III. First use and the risk of war

In considering the risk of war, it is possible to distinguish three different ways in which war might break out.

The type most often discussed is that of 1939—the deliberate act of an aggressive government or ruler: in this case, Hitler. Second, there is the type of 1914: failures in crisis management led to a war that nobody really wanted. Third, there is the Japanese attack of 1941, when Japan judged (wrongly, as it turned out) that a pre-emptive attack might be the last chance for the survival of the Japanese empire in East Asia.

The danger of the third type of outbreak depends upon the foreign and armament policies. The arms race, especially if it is partly successful, is the best way to make this war probable. First-use policy *and* improvements to conventional armaments, which in principle are also appropriate for attack, lead to such an arms race.

The second type of outbreak, the 'guns of August' type,[4] is the most probable in the bipolar world of today, where every conflict all over the world threatens to become a superpower confrontation.[5]

In such a confrontation, the danger is greater if there is a considerable advantage to be obtained from a pre-emptive attack, and if one side believes that the other intends to put into effect any military threats that may have been made. Both these conditions exist with the combination of a first-use policy and conventional dual purpose forces, since a first-use policy is only effective as a deterrent if the adversary believes that it would be put into effect.

On the other hand, a defensive network of conventional forces provides no premium for a pre-emptive attack or a first strike: it is essentially stabilizing.

There remains to be discussed the first type of outbreak, the deliberate attack. This tends to be the only type of outbreak discussed in the West—a deliberate attack by the Soviet Union. It is the only one of the three cases where it could be argued that the first-use option acts as a deterrent. However, there are strong counter-arguments.

First, there is the suicidal nature of such a threat if ever it had to be implemented.

Second, the first-use strategy leads to a local nuclear and conventional arms race, and makes it impossible for any agreement to be reached on levels of strategic nuclear weapons. So the confrontation between the two blocs is exacerbated.

Third, even if NATO adopts a military structure which does not depend on the first use of nuclear weapons, the WTO might still fear the *possibility* of first use.[6] So some deterrent value remains.

Fourth, a deliberate attack can also be deterred by an effective defensive strategy, which makes it impossible for an attacker to achieve his objectives. This form of deterrence is more reliable than deterrence by the potentially suicidal threat of first use. This new idea is now widely accepted in Europe.[7] It is also the basic idea behind General Rogers' proposal for reforming the structure of NATO's conventional forces.

In conclusion, a no-first-use policy for NATO requires that NATO's conventional forces be improved by developing a purely defensive network. Two very important favourable consequences will follow. First, an arms race can be avoided. Second, the risk of war will be less than it is today—taking into account the three different ways (as shown in 1914, 1939 and 1941) in which war can break out.

Notes and references

1. Kissinger, H., 'Strategy and the Atlantic Alliance', *Survival*, Vol. 24, No. 5, September/October 1982, p. 195.
2. The study group of the Max-Plank-Institut zur Erforschung der Lebensbedingungen der wissenschaftlich-technischen Welt in Starnberg was a small group of 10–15 scientists, soldiers and technicians. The model is described in Afheldt, H., *Defensive Verteidigung* (Rowohlt, Reinbek–Hamburg, 1983).
3. Rogers, B. W., 'The Atlantic Alliance. Prescriptions for a difficult decade', *Foreign Affairs*, Summer 1982, pp. 1145–56.
4. This kind of outbreak is described in Tuchman, B. W., *August 1914* (Macmillan, London, 1962).
5. At the end of the 1950s Kissinger described how the intractability of diplomacy has been magnified by the polarization of power after World War II. See Kissinger, H., *The Necessity for Choice. Prospects of American Foreign Policy* (Harper & Row, New York, 1961).
6. This argument is raised in Bundy, McG. *et al.*, 'Nuclear weapons and the Atlantic Alliance', reproduced in this book, pages 29–41.
7. A leading German military journalist wrote that "Security policy through deterrence will have to be continued in the near future. It is impossible to change . . . strategic basic ideas over night. But it is possible to deter the enemy too, in presenting him a military defense system, that is able to resist against any attack . . .". Weinstein, A., *Frankfurter Allgemeine Zeitung*, 5 November 1982, p. 12.

Paper 2. The no-first-use debate and the theory of thresholds

Lawrence Freedman
Professor of War Studies, King's College, University of London, UK

I. Introduction

Few issues irritate the NATO establishment more than the question of no-first-use of nuclear weapons. It puts it on the defensive right from the start, having to argue that NATO is not more reckless than the USSR when it comes to putting the future of civilization at risk to support narrow strategic interests. The issue would only arise, it is pointed out, if the USSR had already taken the gravest possible step and embarked on a full-scale invasion of western Europe. One set of critics has to be reassured that first nuclear use does not mean 'first strike', in that it would be on a limited scale, would involve no attempt to inflict a decisive military victory but would merely warn the aggressor of the consequences of a failure to withdraw. Then it becomes necessary to explain to another set of critics why ever NATO would contemplate such a dangerous move if it could not be relied upon to turn the military tide in its favour. Attempts to counter Soviet propaganda by arguing that no-first-use declarations are virtually useless, especially when made by Moscow, encourage cynicism as to the worth of all rules of conduct that might govern relations between states.

The actual merits of the arguments over NATO strategy tend to get obscured by the awkwardness surrounding the question of first use when posed in a declaratory form. The issue is less one for external pronouncements and more a matter to be decided internally within NATO—it touches upon the responsibilities of government both for the security of its own people and to account for what is done in their name. If NATO is being forced to address the question of its dependence on the threat of first use of nuclear weapons, this is because it has lost the domestic consensus to sustain this threat.

However, the readjustment in doctrine towards a strengthening of the conventional component in deterrence that many would like to see is not one that necessarily lends itself to a pact with the USSR or a promise to the international community. To actually declare a commitment to no-first-use would, in this sense, be icing on the cake. Declaratory policy can rarely be taken as an adequate guide to probable strategy in either crisis or war. The position is likely to be different from that anticipated at a time of relative peace. NATO puts great stress on the threat of first use, yet there are many indications that the firebreak between conventional and nuclear warfare is firmly entrenched in the minds of Alliance leaders who are unwilling to accept the logic of the first-use threat. On the other hand, a commitment to no-first-use might also be misleading. The firebreak is only firmly established in strategic and political theory. There can be no guarantee that it would survive in war whatever the solemn promises made in peace-time, simply because the actual processes of escalation may well be substantially different from those anticipated prior to hostilities. More to the point it would be surprising if any nation did assume that a war among the major powers could avoid 'going nuclear' and it would be utterly irresponsible for them to assume otherwise.

To develop these points further it is argued in this paper that there is a widely agreed framework in which this and related issues are discussed. This framework is influential in thinking about deterrence yet is probably quite invalid as a guide to the likely course of any conflict. It is based on an over-systematic notion of escalation which fails to take adequate account of the dynamics of conflict. It is the uncertain nature of these dynamics that gives strength to the notion of deterrence rather than the specifics of the conditional threats that each side makes against the other. An attempt to introduce certainty—in the direction of either use or non-use of nuclear weapons—is therefore misleading and unhelpful to the maintenance of general deterrence. It is unlikely that means can be found to either inject credibility into nuclear threats or to devise rules of warfare that can guarantee that nuclear weapons will not be employed.

At issue, therefore, is not so much what to promise on nuclear use, but whether any promises can be made at all. We will start our examination of this issue by considering the dominant framework within which much contemporary strategic debate takes place. This framework argues that within each war there are clear and pre-determined moments of decisive political choice as to a war's future course. The disputes are over the nature of these exact moments and the relevant choices at the time.

II. The framework for strategic debate

The framework is based on the concept of escalation, by which any conflict is presumed to be subject to intrinsic expansive tendencies, and is made up of a series of distinct thresholds. These thresholds, when passed, involve the trans-formation of the conflict in the direction of greater violence that is more widely spread and less easily stopped. The passing of each threshold is assumed to have, at the same time, both military and political connotations.

Four key thresholds make regular appearances in the strategic debate:

1. From peace to war (normally assumed to be marked by a large-scale conventional invasion across the East–West divide).

2. From conventional war to nuclear war (the first nuclear weapons employed being those of a shorter range designed for use in and around a battlefield).

3. From continental nuclear to intercontinental nuclear war (i.e., from a conflict confined to the European theatre to one involving the territories of both superpowers).

4. From counterforce to countervalue intercontinental strikes (i.e., from attacks on military sites such as missile silos or submarine pens to attacks directed at the socio-economic structure of the other side).

At issue is whether these thresholds also represent natural firebreaks, that is, whether opposing forces are not driven over them simply as a consequence of the dynamics of war (or involuntary escalation) or whether the passage requires deliberate political decision (voluntary escalation). Particular weapons are often discussed in terms of whether they support or undermine the setting up of firebreaks. For example, the enhanced radiation weapon (the neutron bomb) was both criticized and promoted as something that might blur the line between conventional and nuclear weapons. An important question concerning cruise missiles is whether they inevitably take a conflict into the realm of superpower exchange or whether they would still allow for the confrontation to be contained in the European theatre. The anxiety over ICBM (intercontinental ballistic missile) vulnerability to a surprise Soviet attack, which has much exercised US policymakers over the past decade, revolves around the possibility of a large-scale attack against targets in North America which would be recognized to be something less than all-out nuclear war.

These thresholds are as important as political constraints, whatever their relation to military practice. If they are believed to be real they are real in their consequences. In a nuclear age without, fortunately, much experience to draw upon it is not surprising that anxiety surrounds what potential belligerents *think* they can do as much as what they actually *can* do. Many worry about US policymakers purportedly planning a limited nuclear war not because they themselves are convinced that such a war could be contained within geographic limits but because they believe that the USA might act upon that assumption.

Once a firebreak is established the question becomes one of the factors that influence the political decision as to whether or not to pass over it. It is generally assumed that, all things being equal, there are absolutely no incentives to escalate for the sake of fighting at a higher level, so the causes of escalation must be found in those things which are not equal—the side taking the fateful decision expects either to lose if it does not escalate and/or to win if it does. Thus NATO insists that it would only be the prospect of conventional defeat which would make escalation to the nuclear level conceivable and that, if it were in a less disadvantageous military position to cope with an invasion, then the nuclear threshold would naturally be raised. Alternatively, a positive reason for escalation might be found if it were believed that at the next stage all the advantages would flow in one direction. Hence the fear of a first strike by which all the strength in the earlier stages of a conflict is negated by a successful disarming attack which removes nuclear capabilities.

The final point about this framework for debate is the interrelationship between the different thresholds. If one side is aware that the other is likely to dominate more as escalation proceeds then it will wish to keep the conflict at as low a level as possible. The most important interrelationship is between the first stage, which is the move from peace to war, and assumptions concerning the various stages thereafter. What is thought about the possibility of establishing firebreaks is vital to any decision to initiate war because this is the key determinant of risk. If a war will stay well away from your territory it looks a more attractive proposition than if your cities would be bombed within minutes of the start of hostilities.

III. Firebreaks and the superpowers

It is generally reckoned that the superpowers have the greatest interest in establishing firebreaks. This interest is more or less ordained by the framework which defines the highest stage of the process of escalation as counter-city superpower exchanges. In Washington and Moscow anything is better than that, even though the alternatives may not look strikingly more attractive in either Bonn or Warsaw. The more firebreaks that exist, the greater the chance to contain a conflict at a tolerable level of violence.

The Soviet Union does not employ the language of escalation and thresholds in its strategic literature but there is no doubt that it does recognize thresholds, if not necessarily in exactly the same form as they are viewed in the West. The promotion of the no-first-use issue is in itself an unsurprising acknowledgement of the conventional/nuclear threshold. There is also a distinction made between weapons that can land on Soviet territory and those that cannot. The preoccupation in arms control talks with F-4 aircraft, which have the theoretical range but little practical capacity for attacks on the USSR, is one example of this, as is the comparative lack of interest in the Pershing I which can only hit Soviet allies as against the Pershing II which can reach the USSR.

US strategic thinking has been dominated by the identification of thresholds, often quite contrived, and attempts to assess their significance, often quite fanciful. European observers of this debate have taken slight interest in the threshold that has exercised a powerful hold on the US strategic imagination in the 1970s and 1980s—that between counterforce and countervalue attacks by the superpowers on each other. The fact that the USSR could conceivably find it easier to prevail without crossing this threshold has been held to constitute the sort of advantage that could bring about dramatic political dividends. The USSR might not be able to disarm the USA completely by a counterforce attack but, lacking an ability to respond in kind, the USA would be forced to escalate to counter-city exchanges or else concede defeat. Until the USA had improved the survivability and counterforce capabilities of its own systems, the USSR would enjoy a 'window of opportunity'. That is, it would sense a greater freedom of political manoeuvre than the USA because of a greater confidence in its ability to prevail in most types of confrontation.

Europeans have, by and large, been less agitated by this sort of concern, doubting whether in terms of damage or casualties a counterforce attack would be experienced as being much different from a counter-city attack. The European concern has focused on the earlier thresholds which move a conflict from the conventional to the nuclear and then from the continental to the intercontinental. The USA is perceived as having a clear interest in preventing either threshold from being crossed. Hence the European opposition in the 1960s to the explicit US determination to establish a firebreak between conventional and nuclear warfare and the more recent alarm over what is suspected to be a surreptitious US attempt to ensure that any East–West confrontation is confined to the European theatre. The fear is that if these firebreaks can be established then either superpower will find war a less dangerous proposition and so might be more reckless and provocative in its foreign policy. For Europeans, once the peace/war threshold has been passed the consequences will be catastrophic, so that their interest lies in removing the firebreaks so that there is a clear risk of inexorable escalation attached to the start of any war. Henry Kissinger has even suggested that the Europeans secretly want an immediate jump from conventional to intercontinental nuclear warfare with only a minimal intermediate stage, so that the superpowers would be fighting above the Europeans' heads.

IV. No-first-use

Strategic analysis based on this framework involves the interaction between assumptions concerning the interests of the various parties to any conflict in upholding or undermining particular firebreaks and the technical and practical factors bearing on their ability to do so. For example, the US concern to establish the conventional/nuclear firebreak in the 1960s stemmed from a pessimism as to the possibility of holding on to other thresholds once that one had been passed. Exposition of limited nuclear war theory suggests that current precise and small-yield nuclear weapons facilitate both the blurring of the nuclear threshold and the accentuating of the intercontinental threshold.

The no-first-use debate readily fits into this framework. Those defending NATO's current dependence on the first nuclear use threat are concerned that renunciation of this threat could succeed in creating a firebreak. This, to quote former US Secretary of State Alexander Haig, would "make Europe safe for conventional aggression."[1] The conventional forces available to the Alliance, it is argued, are insufficient now to cope with a determined WTO invasion and there is no reason to believe that this position will be improved decisively in the coming years. Therefore the USSR need not be deterred by thought of failure in any expansionist enterprise. Nor need it be deterred by the thought of suffering excessive costs—without nuclear use there could be no direct threat to Soviet territory. So with prospective gains substantial and prospective costs limited, the Soviet leaders could contemplate war from their sanctuary in Moscow with something approaching equanimity. By contrast, the people of central Europe could only be appalled by the prospect: their lands would be ravaged and their way of life ruined forever. Certainly the peoples of eastern Europe would suffer but, it is presumed, this would not be a decisive factor.

The opponents argue that it is highly unlikely that the Kremlin is only held back by the nuclear threat as this threat is inherently incredible—the firebreak is already firmly in place. There is no form of limited military employment of nuclear weapons that could turn the course of battle in NATO's favour unless the WTO failed to respond in kind—something of a slender reed upon which to rely. To sustain the threat it becomes necessary to develop strategies to make it easier to use nuclear weapons, but the attempt to do this has so far failed. In all probability, once nuclear weapons had been used escalation would be rapid. Meanwhile, even 'limited' use would be dreadful for those purportedly being defended. Use beyond the battlefield would certainly wound the USSR, perhaps mortally, but the same would be true for all of NATO. Once nuclear weapons come into use NATO's position can never be improved. The only alternative is to recognize the inevitable and work within the limits imposed by this natural firebreak, and improve conventional deterrence while ensuring that the USSR is never tempted into nuclear escalation by maintaining a secure second-strike capability.

V. Theory into practice—some scenarios

Deterrence depends on the views held on the likely course of a conflict. The extent to which, and conviction with which, these views are held are therefore more important than their connection with reality. Moreover, reality is something impossible to establish in this instance without experiencing it, so one person's guess is as good as that of another. This particular framework is found valuable because it imposes some order on what would otherwise be a mass of uncertainties, it reflects much modern thinking which sees conflict as a series of graduated steps (often judging harshly those responsible for moving from one to the other) while also accommodating strikingly different political views. The framework's attractions are very much in evidence in the terms in which the no-first-use debate is phrased. Something so influential that defies invalidation should only be confronted with respect and caution. It must, however, be confronted if we are to put the no-first-use debate into perspective.

The framework involves more than a series of steps moving in one clear direction—of increasing violence and destructiveness. It also involves considerations of type of target (military/civilian) and geographical scope. It suggests that the order of gravity of the various steps, once hostilities have begun, is to move from conventional to nuclear munitions, then to move from a central European theatre to superpower exchanges, and finally from military to civilian targets. The latter two steps, of course, only acquire their particular gravity because the nuclear step has already been taken.

But the identification and ordering of strategic choices within this framework reflects more than anything else the current, peace-time political debate within NATO. That is, the framework is shaped by understandings of the risks that the various members of NATO feel it right for them to take. This does not mean that this framework will bear much relation to the choices that they would actually face in war. There has always been great interest in the possibility of a nuclear first-strike which would see the peace/war, conventional/nuclear and continental/intercontinental thresholds passed in one dramatic surprise attack. A successful first strike is now probably not feasible. As this was always the only compelling military scenario for the crossing of the nuclear threshold then it may be that more of the vital choices will be faced within the conventional phase. There is no reason in principle why the geographical expansion of the war or the deliberate inclusion of civilian targets might not take place before the nuclear threshold has been passed. Indeed if the enormity of the passing of these thresholds derives largely from an assumption of the war having already 'gone nuclear', then it may be easier to pass them if the war is still at a conventional level.

It is easy enough to see how civilians might get involved early in any war in central Europe. Many urban areas would soon be in combat zones and civilians, either caught in their homes or fleeing as refugees, could soon appear as military obstacles. At some point a target whose destruction is essential to the military effort will appear in the middle of a civilian population, or measures ostensibly intended to harm enemy forces, such as opening dams, will cause immense civilian harm. It is less easy to explain a pre-nuclear expansion of a conflict to superpower territory, because the main means of this expansion are nuclear weapons, although some nuclear-capable systems such as heavy bombers could be used with conventional munitions. However, there are other critical forms of geographical expansion, rarely touched on in public debate within NATO except in the countries concerned. Even confined to Europe there will be important questions of policy, possibly initially facing the USSR more than the West, concerning the involvement of either Scandinavian countries or those of southern Europe. There will be temptations to violate the neutrality of Austria, Sweden or Yugoslavia. On the Western side, the questions may arise of punitive, but non-nuclear, measures against the satellite countries of eastern Europe. If a stalemate develops along the central front then the movement of reserves and raw materials will become crucial, turning the conflict into more of a naval affair. Here the possibilities for geographical expansion become immense.

It is also possible to imagine other moves which might appear as serious escalation at the time which do not figure prominently in peace-time calculations: whether to use forms of chemical weapon, to attack economic assets such as energy installations, to engage in combat with forces from countries that might be persuaded to play only a small role in the fighting. Moreover, contrary to the expectations created by the concept of escalation the various thresholds do not appear in a logical sequence along some unilinear path. The difficulty in predicting the course of any war lies in the difficulty in projecting military moves beyond the first few.

Examining a country's strategic position in peace-time enables the sort of objectives that are likely to impress themselves upon its planners to be identified. We may then be able to make a considered judgement as to how the potential enemy will seek to frustrate the achievement of those objectives. Identification of either side's fall-back plans is less easy and beyond that the task is impossible.

Much of the discussion of NATO doctrine assumes that in the first week of war a WTO invasion will be clearly succeeding, in which case NATO will have to consider nuclear use, or it will have failed, in which case the Kremlin will have to negotiate an honourable retreat. Either is possible, but so is something in between—only partial success or failure, with NATO grimly holding on or a Soviet attack faltering with both sides desperate to find some way of breaking the impasse without resort to nuclear weapons. Or if NATO repels the first Soviet thrust, the temptation may be to take the war into Eastern territory. In these circumstances the war could take many forms, each alternative reflecting a different combination of political compromise and military judgement.

Even if we take just one type of escalation, that of increasing levels of violence, the model appears inadequate. Military campaigns do not necessarily begin with small skirmishes and end with a crescendo in a great clash of armies. The first engagements may be the bloodiest or some set-piece attack designed to make a political point with few casualties can go terribly wrong and lead to tremendous loss of life.

Thus, within the conventional phase there are large numbers of thresholds that might or might not be passed, voluntarily or involuntarily, before the issue of nuclear use need arise. The same is not necessarily true once the nuclear threshold has been passed. By that I mean it is less easy to establish clear firebreaks that separate types of nuclear war from each other. For practical reasons the continental/intercontinental may be one such threshold, but there are obvious means by which it might be passed despite a deliberate intention not to do so. Attacks on US nuclear bases in Europe or nuclear-weapon-carrying aircraft carriers or submarines might be ambiguous in their meaning. The proximity of the USSR to the likely combat area means that it could prove difficult to avoid an attack against WTO supply lines spilling over into Soviet territory. Distinctions between civilian and military targets appear as extremely difficult to sustain. The civilian casualties resulting from a so-called counterforce attack against US military installations would only be 'limited' when compared with what might have resulted from a dedicated counter-city attack, but certainly not by comparison with anything in US experience. Attempts to conduct controlled and selective strikes are at any rate liable to frustration by the collapse of systems for command and control as well as by the difficulty of establishing understood, agreed and unambiguous rules of engagement for nuclear war.

It is often supposed that the crossing of the nuclear threshold would be marked by tentative, demonstrative, small-scale and small-yield nuclear detonations. This cannot be ruled out as there are no certainties in this area. But there are reasonable grounds for assuming that the incentives with any early nuclear blow would be to achieve the maximum military impact, possibly on the assumption that this would also bring about the maximum political impact. A restrained nuclear attack might fail to turn a deteriorating military position while removing inhibitions on enemy nuclear use. Furthermore, if we again assume that passing the nuclear threshold will only happen as the result of utter desperation then the manner of the passage is likely to bear all the hallmarks of desperation. (The converse of this might be that early and non-desperate passage of the nuclear threshold would allow for the sort of stylized nuclear bargaining envisaged in some of the textbooks.)

VI. Conclusions

The thrust of this argument has been to cast doubt on the general theory of firebreaks, as over-systematic and failing to do justice to the number and character of the thresholds that will face political and military leaders in the conventional phase while exaggerating the possibilities for distinct stages in the nuclear phase. In this the specific validity of the concentration on the conventional/nuclear firebreak has also been accepted.

This firebreak is now part of our strategic culture, political practice and military preparations. Whatever the claims of the doctrine, NATO is organized so as to ensure that passing this threshold would be a deliberate political decision. This can be seen in the guidelines for consultation on nuclear use, the special command structure controlling nuclear weapons, the promises made when the issue of threshold-transcending weapons, such as 'mini-nukes', have arisen and the general treatment of nuclear matters in public debate. It is likely that in a really serious international crisis the stress on this firebreak would intensify. The necessity of sustaining a domestic consensus would involve reassurances on the limited nature of the risks in taking a firm stand.

Does this mean that the firebreak would hold up to the actual pressures of war? It is impossible to be dogmatic on this question. In the end it is a matter of judgement. Experience from World War II provides no clear-cut answer. The no-first-use pact on chemical and biological weapons did hold, but this is generally believed to result from the limited military utility of these weapons as well as the fear of retaliation. It now seems that Churchill did actively consider their use as a counter to the V-weapons, but in the end was dissuaded. In the case of air raids on cities the war started with both sides anxious to avoid such raids, largely because of the fear of retaliation, but these inhibitions failed to hold—air raids *were* believed to be of military value.

If this experience suggests anything it is that the question of military utility will be decisive. The proponents of no-first-use declarations tend now to argue their case on the lack of any tangible benefit to be gained by employment of nuclear weapons as well as on the obvious costs. Under current conditions, with both sides always able to threaten retaliation to any initial nuclear use, it is very hard to see any military incentives arguing for such escalation. On the other hand, it is also hard to see the point of any break of the nuclear taboo being solely for

75

political purposes, without regard to political considerations. If it is a desperate situation in land combat that prompts consideration of nuclear use, then it seems likely that the incentive will be to make some attempt to improve the military position. This is unlikely to argue for limited employment. Something tentative may serve no military purpose while failing to signal political resolve. To make matters worse, the taboo having been broken the enemy may feel uninhibited in response. The circumstances, opportunities and probable repercussions of the first nuclear volley of a war are likely to encourage the full exploitation of this dramatic gamble.

All this suggests that the firebreak will exercise a firm hold on policy-makers within war and that there will be little inclination to violate it. But this is not the same as saying that the threshold is inviolable. Circumstances might arise of extreme desperation or of a sudden military opportunity. Or else there could just be some dreadful failure of control, with one of those accidents that gain publicity in peace-time but are never really dangerous because of the incredulity of those responsible when receiving signals of impending attack, turning into a nightmare.

This leaves us with a paradoxical but not necessarily contradictory position: in the event of war the overwhelming disposition of all the belligerents would be to avoid passing the nuclear threshold but, nevertheless, because of the extreme pressures to which the firebreak would be subjected, it cannot be assumed that it would not be passed. This would be true whether declarations of no-first-use had been made or not.

The final question is whether assumptions on the likelihood or otherwise of this threshold being passed will affect the most important threshold between peace and war. One of the problems in answering this question is the generally hazy actions concerning this threshold, despite intensive analysis of the concept of crisis management. This is largely because of the welcome difficulty in conceiving of plausible scenarios for the outbreak of an East–West war. This in turn is a result of the apparently fixed nature of the East–West political divide. If war comes it is likely to be as a result of some disruption to these political arrangements, in which case the overall situation will be messy and the move from peace to war more prolonged and less decisive than is often imagined. Any military action will, in the first instance, be taken in the belief that the consequences will be limited and manageable. The most influential thresholds would then be those in the conventional sphere. The key questions would be political—for example, what do I need to do to restore the *status quo ante* and how can I do this without drawing into the conflict too many of my potential enemies.

In crises the incentives will be to convey a vague sense of dire threat to the enemy while searching for ways to keep risks limited for one's own side. As noted earlier, this is the interest of the superpowers. In NATO, the need to limit the apparent liability may well be a prerequisite for alliance cohesion. Thus the political decisions behind preparations for war, and even early hostilities, will involve a tension between calculations of the specific costs and benefits of the 'next step' and a general unease concerning where it all might lead. Some critical moves, for example the transportation of reserves or movement of naval forces, may result from a recognition that unless taken, defensive capabilities will perish through neglect. There is no reason to believe that the sense of a deteriorating military position will influence the passage across the peace/war threshold any less than across the conventional/nuclear threshold. The risk is therefore of an immediate military logic—possibly the old logic of mobilization and temptations to pre-empt—forcing the pace of a dispute.

In these circumstances of escalation within the conventional sphere then the worry that the conflict could somehow go nuclear might introduce a vital note of caution. So long as the major powers have nuclear weapons it is vital that this note be introduced, not only to calm immediate pressures to war but because, with the dynamics of modern war so imperfectly understood, this note may well be entirely justified. There have been a number of crises in recent decades where realistic strategic analysis could see no possible incentives to use nuclear weapons even though the superpowers could get involved in a direct confrontation. A no-first-use declaration would have seemed redundant yet prudence still dictated holding back from any form of direct clash.

The proponents of no-first-use declarations have confused the need to unburden NATO of a threat of first use, which is militarily incredible, politically divisive and morally disreputable, by substituting something equally definite in its place. A promise of non-nuclear war is no more credible, uniting or moral. The first conclusion of this analysis is that war is so indeterminate that no firm predictions can be made as to its likely course and that therefore no established limitations, even if acceptable and desirable to both sides, can be guaranteed to hold. The second conclusion is that the preoccupation with the conventional/nuclear threshold leaps over the great variety of alternative forms that a conventional war might take. The need to suspect the optimism behind the notion of non-nuclear war between nuclear powers must be matched by the development of a keener political understanding of the nature of non-nuclear war.

Reference
[1] *New York Times*, 7 April 1982, p. 4.

Paper 3.   Alternatives to the first use of nuclear weapons

Daniel Frei
Professor of Political Science, University of Zurich, Switzerland

I. Introduction

It is a truism that the principle of a possible first use of nuclear weapons, which underlies NATO's strategy of 'flexible response', has a number of strategic, political, and, last but not least, ethical shortcomings. However, this does not necessarily mean that the simple antonym of first use, that is, the adoption of a commitment to no-first-use, would automatically remedy all of them. As a matter of fact, there are many more alternatives to first use[1] than a mere no-first-use pledge, as figure 3.1 suggests. (The alternatives examined here are printed in *italics*.) The following contribution first briefly identifies some of the problems that would still be left unsolved after a hypothetical adoption of an unqualified no-first-use pledge. Second, it tries to examine some major alternatives to both first use *and* unqualified no-first-use.

Figure 3.1.   Alternatives to first use

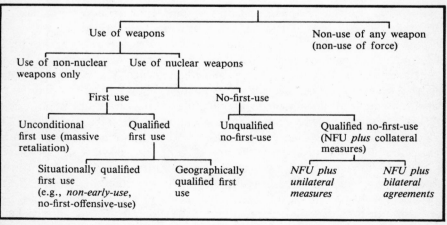

NFU = no-first-use.

II. *The riddle of a no-first-use pledge* pur et simple

Assuming NATO were to adopt a commitment to unqualified no-first-use, that is, no-first-use *pur et simple*, leaving unchanged any other aspects of the strategic postures and the political order—what problems would remain unsolved or, worse, would even be aggravated? Among the various problems mentioned in this context three major ones deserve serious consideration: (*a*) the effectiveness of NATO's deterrence posture; (*b*) the reliability of US security guarantees for western Europe; and (*c*) the meaning and value of a mutual no-first-use pledge within the framework of the contemporary East–West confrontation.

1. While NATO's concept of 'flexible response' is based on the maintenance of uncertainty about a possible first use of nuclear weapons, a no-first-use commitment makes the response predictable, and according to some observers even "predictably inadequate",[2] as a potential aggressor now can rely on being relieved of the risk of nuclear retaliation.[3] Certainty about a limited, calculable response may invite aggression[4] and thus increase the risk of war. This last conclusion may indeed be questioned: what is less questionable is the widely accepted fact that uncertainty at least induces caution on the part of a potential aggressor and thus contributes to strengthening deterrence because even quite a small possibility of catastrophe may be enough to deter an attack.[5] This ultimate consequence of the flexible response strategy is valid despite the delicate credibility problems it involves and despite considerable disagreement about the costs of this strategy, especially about the cost if deterrence should fail. If NATO undertook an unqualified no-first-use pledge, this would obviously affect the deterrence function and, by implication, also the other two functions which the strategy of flexible response aims to fulfill, that is, defence by delay, and the reduction of Soviet political leverage by limiting the effectiveness of Soviet military force as an instrument of political coercion.[6]

2. There are growing credibility problems about security guarantees of the USA to its European allies; consequently an increasing amount of attention is given to the strategic coupling of European and US territory. Practically all Western experts tend to agree that US nuclear weapons stationed in Europe as a 'leg' of NATO's retaliatory force "guarantee that, if there is a war in Europe, it will couple the American nuclear defence to European nuclear defence".[7] Their view is fully shared by authoritative Soviet statements; Marshal Ustinov and Marshal Ogarkov have repeatedly stressed that "Soviet strategic forces are capable of launching an immediate, annihilating counter-strike against any target of the globe once an enemy employs nuclear weapons against the Soviet Union or other countries of the socialist community".[8] Advocates of no-first-use point to the desirability of introducing 'firebreaks' into the process of automatic escalation—however, "firebreaks are the very antithesis of coupling".[9] In the absence of any collateral measure, and only under this condition, a no-first-use commitment *pur et simple*, by constituting such a firebreak, would necessarily jeopardize or even destroy the credibility of the ultimate US guarantee behind

extended deterrence. It is hard to deny that such a step would therefore drastically undermine the credibility of NATO's deterrent and thus again increase the risk of war rather than reduce it.

3. The most serious flaw of a no-first-use pledge *pur et simple* of course is its questionable reliability. A mere pledge, being nothing but a declaratory policy, constitutes no substitute for a guarantee. What does a pledge referring to the renunciation of a type of action (i.e., first use) mean while the capability for executing this very action is not removed? As long as the capability for launching a second strike exists, how can anyone credibly prove the absence of intention to use nuclear weapons first? The present conventional and nuclear confrontation in Europe obviously has roots in a situation characterized by conflict, distrust and fear—why should a simple pledge be trusted?[9] After all, the reliability problems of a no-first-use pledge are identical with those of any so-called "negative security assurance",[10] which for the same reason, and in the absence of true nuclear disarmament, also fails to be convincing. One may even question whether no-first-use would serve as a gesture to initiate a process of relaxation of tension on a reciprocal basis. A no-first-use pledge without adequate provisions for an alternative security arrangement might on the contrary provoke all kinds of undesirable reactions, such as misunderstandings and miscalculations by the other side; it might serve as an incentive to nuclear proliferation on the part of those allies who have to forego the nuclear guarantee.[11]

Apart from these general considerations there are also more specific reasons why no-first-use *pur et simple* cannot but go awry. As far as NATO is concerned, the number of nuclear-capable systems, especially the number of aircraft, exceeds the number of long-range theatre ballistic missiles and cruise missiles which usually catch the main share of attention.[12] Recent Soviet indications point to considerable anxieties about these systems. Furthermore, Soviet sources often refer to concepts of launch-under-attack and even launch-on-warning;[13] these concepts do not differ much from a posture of "striking first in the last resort".[14] At least it is fair to say that the WTO has no guarantee that a hypothetical no-first-use pledge by NATO will be reliable—hence it will act accordingly.

Similar and maybe more explicit fears prevail in the West, founded on three particular aspects of Soviet strategic doctrine and force deployment. The first aspect has to do with the Marxist–Leninist notion of the 'correlation of forces' which somehow contrasts with the Western concepts of 'balance' or 'stability': according to the Soviet view, "the constant expansion of the socialist system, and the prevention of a world war in our time, have been achieved thanks to the dynamic of the correlation of world forces and its change in favour of socialism".[15] The second aspect is the emphasis on surprise and deception in Soviet theory: it is reflected in the notion of striking "at the most favorable moment" and in the importance of concepts such as *maskirova* (camouflage, deception) and *dezinformatsiya* (misinformation).[16] The third aspect arises from the offensive concept of the Soviet defence posture: the key element in Soviet doctrine is the *Blitzkrieg*-type operation whose objective is to keep the initiative by massive offensive operations, if deterrence fails.[17]

These three aspects of Soviet doctrine and force deployment, in conjunction with actual Soviet capabilities for launching a first strike against western Europe, and taking also into account the range of Soviet SS-20 missiles, are hardly conducive to producing a feeling in the West that Soviet no-first-use pledges have a high degree of credibility and reliability. In conclusion, a no-first-use pledge *pur et simple* leaves open the crucial dilemma inherent in any unqualified disarmament or arms control measure: how to detect non-compliance in time and how to react once a violation occurs. The key problem is to find working alternatives to first use, or, to put it in the careful wording of the Pugwash Council, "the removal of the obstacles which keep all countries possessing nuclear weapons from declaring their intention not to use these weapons first".[18]

III. Alternatives to first use and unqualified no-first-use

When looking for alternatives to both the doctrines of first use and unqualified no-first-use, the optimal solution would be a mutual pledge not to use, under any circumstances, nuclear and conventional weapons, that is, a treaty on the non-use of force. Such a treaty has been repeatedly proposed by the Soviet Union and her allies;[19] however, the provisions of the Charter of the United Nations, especially article 2, paragraph 4 ("All Members shall refrain in their international relations from the threat or use of force . . ."), and of the 1975 Final Act of the Conference on Security and Co-operation in Europe (CSCE), already basically fulfill this demand. The failure to implement these provisions again suggests that the problem of security cannot be solved by any paper substitute such as a pledge, a treaty or a charter. As this way out of the dilemma is impractical, one has to look into no-first-use concepts supplemented by collateral measures.

The most salient proposal, incorporating a collateral measure, aims at substituting the threat to use nuclear weapons first by strengthening NATO's conventional defence. Some authors argue that NATO's prospects for thwarting a Soviet offensive are already now quite good[20]—provided the Soviet Union does not choose to attack by using nuclear weapons first,[21] in which case conventional weapons would be useless. Other authors assume that Western superiority in weapon technology (especially in the field of precision-guided munitions and anti-tank missiles), coupled with a concerted agreement to increase national defence budgets by 3–4.5 per cent a year (in volume), would be sufficient to deter Soviet attack and would assure effective defence if deterrence fails.[22] The majority of experts, however, conclude that reliance on purely conventional deterrence and defence represents no panacea.[23] The point here is not to find out which of the two positions receives broader expert support; the divergence in expert opinion simply serves to show that there is uncertainty about the value of reinforced conventional defence as a substitute for the first use of nuclear weapons. With such a degree of uncertainty, it seems unlikely that any responsible statesman in the West would seriously consider, let alone embark on, such a course. Even if this solution were feasible, two serious flaws remain. First, there is the fear that in view of the destructive power of modern conventional weapons, the consequences of conventional defence would be almost indistinguishable from the consequences of nuclear warfare in Europe.[24] Second, the advocates of a strong reinforcement of NATO's conventional capabilities tend to neglect the problem of the political acceptability of such a step; the other side may easily perceive it as a major provocation, especially in view of a potential strategic first-strike use of the new long-range 'smart' weapons[25] which might be targeted against command, control and communications centres.

Still, the idea of upgrading NATO's conventional capabilities should not be entirely rejected. It is useful and highly desirable if it contributes to raising the nuclear threshold and thus helps to transform the traditional first-use concept into the principle of non-early-use of nuclear weapons. According to present NATO doctrine, nuclear weapons will be used "as late as possible, however as soon as necessary".[26] Although NATO planners refuse to define the precise location of the nuclear thesbold, with the intention of creating an element of uncertainty, it can be assumed that they are interested in keeping the nuclear threshold as high as possible. Raising it would therefore be a logical continuation of existing policy. In practical terms this would imply three measures: (1) strengthening conventional defence; (2) nuclear de-emphasis, particularly by withdrawing nuclear weapons from the forward edge of the battle area (FEBA) in order to avoid their "automatic" early use according to the principle of "use it or lose it";[27] and (3) giving preference to conventional forces strong in the defensive but weak in the offensive mode.[28] These measures would deliberately fall short of establishing a firebreak between conventional and nuclear weapons, thus maintaining the US–European link constituted by the principle of credible extended deterrence. It is still not clear what this means in terms of actual deployment of US nuclear systems dedicated to the defence of western Europe; for some time very probably the debate will continue whether for instance sea-based nuclear forces (or even US-based Minuteman III missiles) would be 'enough' or whether the actual deployment of nuclear weapons close to the front is required.[29] Obviously, there exists a trade-off between the deterrence value of a forward-based nuclear system due to uncertainty (implying, however, the doomsday perspective of a high risk of escalation overriding any firebreaks) on the one hand, and the raising of the nuclear threshold (implying, however, the risk that a potential aggressor may find the expected costs calculable and possibly also acceptable). Either extreme is clearly unsatisfactory. When looking for a "no-early-use" solution, it is therefore crucial to avoid either extreme and to find the optimum compromise between the two configurations.

It is sometimes argued that the central dilemma of NATO's present doctrine of a possible first use of nuclear weapons is that it may only leave the choice between either inadvertent escalation followed by mutual annihilation or reluctance, on the part of the US president, to honour the US commitment to NATO. If it is not so much the credibility of deterrence *per se* but the credibility of its extension to allies which constitutes the key problem (as assumed in French nuclear policy), then one might ask whether it would not be preferable to generalize the French concept and to decouple west European deterrence from the Atlantic link by setting up a purely European force capable of deterring an attack by conventional and, if necessary, also by nuclear means. However, the idea of a "Europeanized" deterrence must be discarded for at least three reasons.[30] (a) European decision-making in nuclear strategy would presuppose a political infrastructure going far beyond the boldest dreams of European unification; (b) it can hardly be supposed that the two European nuclear powers, France and the UK, would be willing to cede control of their nuclear weapons to an outside decision-centre; and (c) the absence of the threat of retaliation by US strategic forces may reduce the threat exerted by the European deterrent and make it quite limited and at any rate calculable; as a no-first-use pledge made by the Europeans, being nothing but a pledge, lacks reliability, the European nuclear capability might invite a pre-emptive strike by a potential aggressor.

Instead of linking a no-first-use commitment with a reconstruction of the conventional balance by strengthening NATO's conventional forces one might reach the same goal by an arms-control approach. David Owen suggests that "NATO and the Warsaw Pact should set as their first objective a negotiated conventional force balance which would allow the negotiation of a 'limited no first use' of nuclear weapons treaty".[31] One may disagree about whether or not the current Mutual (Balanced) Force Reduction (MBFR) negotiations in Vienna offer the proper framework for such an approach; some aspects central to an eventual reconstruction of the conventional balance in Europe are obviously not on the agenda of the MBFR negotiations.[32] Although this approach seems to be the most promising and rational one, one cannot avoid expressing some reservations. Since this approach would require large concessions from the East, it would hardly be politically feasible. Furthermore, as David Holloway aptly put it, "what is taking place is a competition not only in arms, but also in strategies, with each side seeking to make the strategy of the other unworkable".[33] Recommending "an agreement in Vienna [which] would bring the West an increment of security at no cost"[34] as a collateral measure coupled with a no-first-use pledge presupposes a communality of interests between East and West which simply does not exist.

It is wise to keep this latter reservation in mind when finally examining the meaning of a no-first-use pledge accompanied by confidence-building collateral measures. Ideally confidence-building measures (CBMs) serve the purpose of demonstrating non-aggressive intentions; in times of crisis they allow for early warning and thus preclude a surprise attack.[35] If it were possible to reach agreement about a comprehensive system of CBMs fully covering these two goals, a commitment to no-first-use would make sense, provided the CBMs include everything discussed so far within the context of the CSCE (expansion of the CBMs adopted in Helsinki) and MBFR (so-called "associated measures") and possibly also some additional measures going beyond the present CBM 'regime'. These measures should preferably include also withdrawal by 50 or 100 km or more of all kinds of conventional armament that are perceived to reflect an offensive posture (especially tanks but also modern anti-tank weapons). A broad zone free of offensive weapons (whatever the opponents, in the situation of mutual suspicion, define as "offensive") would be far more important than any type of zone free of nuclear weapons (which, in view of the range available to modern tactical nuclear systems, would be of doubtful value anyway). However, the fate of the many proposals so far submitted for extending existing CBMs suggests that optimism might be premature. In particular it is doubtful whether existing asymmetries in doctrine and deployment could be altered by introducing new CBMs. The political feasibility of any such proposal is limited both by irreconcilable political interests and by the inertia of existing military structures. Deeply embedded doctrines and long-standing traditions of weapon procurement would have to be changed.

IV. Conclusions

Table 3.1 presents a summary tentative evaluation of a no-first-use pledge *pur et simple* and its alternatives, based on the criteria underlying the current debate on East–West strategic relations; the scores used ('good', 'medium' and 'poor') summarize the more refined arguments elaborated above.

Three conclusions suggest themselves:

1. It would seem that on balance the options 'NFU plus strong conventional defence' and 'non-early-use of nuclear weapons' deserve priority. As far as the criterion of political feasibility is concerned, the "non-early-use" option seems to be clearly superior. It therefore can be said to constitute the optimum solution.

2. The present NATO concept of uncertainty about a possible first use of nuclear weapons on the whole does not score badly; yet if the criterion 'political feasibility' is replaced by 'political costs' the picture becomes somewhat different, especially in the light of the current debate about upgrading NATO's TNF arsenal.

Table 3.1. **Tentative evaluation of a no-first-use (NFU) pledge** *pur et simple*

Option	Evaluation			
	Deterrence	Defence	Escalation control (firebreak)	Political feasibility
Present NATO concept	Medium	Good	Poor	(in operation)
NFU *pur et simple*	Poor	Poor	Good	Medium
Non-use of force	Poor	Poor	Good	Poor
NFU plus stronger conventional defence	Medium	Good	Good	Medium
Non-early-use of nuclear weapons	Medium	Good	Medium	Good
NFU plus Europeanization of nuclear deterrent	Poor	Poor	Good	Poor
NFU plus conventional arms control	Medium	Medium	Medium	Medium
NFU plus CBMs	Medium	Good	Medium	Medium

3. The options 'NFU plus CBMs' and 'NFU plus conventional arms control' too seem to be quite favourable, ranking closely behind the options emerging in this table as the optimum solution. This fact strongly suggests that it would be desirable to combine the 'non-early-use' option, to the greatest extent possible, with a CBM and arms control approach. The relevant negotiations deserve to be given new momentum for the sake of mitigating the dangerous dilemma posed by the present strategic confrontation in Europe.

Notes and references

[1] Compare, for some alternatives: Heisenberg, W., *Möglichkeiten und Gefahren nichtmilitärischer Einsatzbeschränkungen für Kernwaffen* (Stiftung Wissenschaft und Politik, Ebenhausen, 1973), pp. 15–24; Newcombe, H., 'Approaches to a nuclear-free future', *Peace Research Reviews*, Vol. 6, No. 2, October 1974, pp. 93–98.

[2] Brzezinski, Z., 'East–West relations: strategic crossroads', *Trialogue*, No. 30/1, Summer/Fall 1982, pp. 18–21.

[3] Kaiser, K. *et al.*, Kernwaffen und die Erhaltung des Friedens', *Europa-Archiv*, Vol. 37, No. 12, June 1982, p. 360.

[4] Kober, S., letter to the editor, *Foreign Affairs*, Vol. 60, No. 5, Summer 1982, p. 1171.

[5] Dessler, D., ' "Just in case"—the danger of flexible response', *Bulletin of the Atomic Scientists*, Vol. 38, No. 9, December 1982, p. 56f; Lodgaard, S., 'Long-range theatre nuclear forces in Europe', in SIPRI, *World Armaments and Disarmament, SIPRI Yearbook 1982* (Taylor & Francis, London, 1982), p. 31f; Speed, R. D., *Strategic Deterrence in the 1980s* (Hoover Institution Press, Stanford, 1979), pp. 106–10; Richelson, J. T., 'Soviet strategic doctrine and limited nuclear operations', *Journal of Conflict Resolution*, Vol. 23, No. 2, June 1979, pp. 326–36; Burrows, B. and Edwards, G., *The Defence of Western Europe* (Butterworth, London, 1982), pp. 100ff; Stratmann, K-P., *NATO-Strategie in der Krise?* (Nomos, Baden-Baden, 1981), p. 229; Voigt, K-D., 'Das Risiko eines begrenzten Nuklearkrieges in Europa', *Europa-Archiv*, Vol. 37, No. 6, March 1982, pp. 151–60. The unanimity of these various sources with respect to the uncertainty/deterrence relationship is quite impressive.

[6] Compare Weinberger, C., *FY 1983 Report of the Secretary of Defense to the Congress* (US Government Printing Office, Washington, D.C., 8 February 1982), Part II, p. 17.

[7] Kissinger, H., 'The international context for US security', *Adelphi Paper No. 174* (IISS, London, 1982), p. 6.

[8] Ogarkov, N. W., in *Kommunist*, No. 10, 1980; Ustinov, D. F., in *The Threat to Europe* (Soviet Committee for European Security and Co-operation, Moscow, 1981), p. 10.

[9] Compare Heisenberg, W., 'Kernwaffen in Europa: Probleme einer vereinbarten Kontrolle', in *Polarität und Interdependenz* (Nomos, Baden-Baden, 1978), pp. 203–17; de Rose, F., 'Inflexible response', *Foreign Affairs*, Vol. 61, No. 1, Fall 1982, p. 138; Makins, C. J., 'TNF modernization and "countervailing strategy" ', *Survival*, Vol. 23, No. 4, July/August 1981, pp. 160f; Ravenal, E. C., letter to the editor, *Foreign Affairs*, Vol. 60, No. 5, Summer 1982, p. 1175. For a more general examination of the security dilemma involved here, compare Frei, D. and Gaupp, P., 'Das Konzept "Sicherheit" ', in Schwarz, K-D. (ed.), *Sicherheits-politik* (Osang,

Baden-Baden, 1979), pp. 3-16.

10 Goldblat, J., *Agreements for Arms Control: A Critical Survey*, SIPRI (Taylor & Francis, London, 1982), p. 46.

11 Geyer, A., *The Idea of Disarmament* (Brethren Press, Elgin, IL, 1982), pp. 174f.

12 Freedman, L., 'The dilemma of theatre nuclear ams control', *Survival*, Vol. 23, No. 1, January/February 1981, pp. 5f; Davis, L. E., 'A proposal for TNF arms control', *Survival*, Vol. 23, No. 6, November/December 1981, pp. 234f; Lunn, S., 'At issue: nuclear modernization in Europe', *Bulletin of the Atomic Scientists*, Vol. 38, No. 7, August/September 1982, p. 21.

13 Ustinov, D., 'To avert the threat of nuclear war', *International Affairs* (Moscow), No. 9, September 1982, pp. 18f; Siegmund, W. and Kleine, J., 'Die gegenwärtige Militärdoktrin der USA—eine flagrante Verletzung des völkerrechtlichen Gebots der Friedenssicherung', *Deutsche Aussenpolitik*, Vol. 27, No. 9, 1982, p. 87.

14 Quoted in Erickson, J., 'The Soviet view of deterrence', *Survival*, Vol. 24, No. 6, November/December 1982, p. 244. Compare also Jones, D. C., letter to the editor, *Foreign Affairs*, Vol. 60, No. 5, Summer 1982, p. 1173.

15 Lider, J., 'The correlation of world forces: the Soviet concept', *Journal of Peace Research*, Vol. 17, No. 2, 1980, p. 156. Compare also Ermath, F. W., 'Contrasts in American and Soviet strategic thought', in Leebaert, D. (ed.), *Soviet Military Thinking* (Allen & Unwin, London, 1981), p. 58f.

16 Valenta, J., 'Soviet use of surprise and deception', *Survival*, Vol. 24, No. 2, March/April 1982, pp. 50-61; Erickson, J., 'The Soviet military potential for surprise attack: surprise, superiority and time', in Pfaltzgraff, R.L., Ra'anan, U. and Milberg, W. (eds), *Intelligence Policy and National Security* (Macmillan, London, 1981), pp. 49-73; Douglass, J. D. and Hoeber, A. M., *Soviet Strategy for Nuclear War* (Hoover Institution Press, Stanford, 1979), pp. 102f.

17 Senghaas, D., 'Bestehen Chancen für erfolgreiche Rüstungskontrollverhandlungen?', in Lutz, D.S. and Gremliza, D. (eds), *Rustung zum Tode?* (Konkret, Hamburg, 1981), pp. 48f; Tiedtke, S., *Rüstungskontrolle aus sowjetischer Sicht* (Campus, Frankfurt, 1980), pp. 66f; Canby, S., 'Military doctrine and technology', in Alford, J. (ed.), *The Impact of New Military Technology* (Gower, London, 1981), p. 13.

18 *Pugwash Newsletter*, Vol. 20, No. 2, October 1982, p. 24.

19 Yefremov, A. Y., *Nuclear Disarmament* (Progress, Moscow, 1976), p. 255; Yefremov, A. Y., *Peace and Disarmament 1980* (Progress, Moscow, 1980), p. 153; Kende, I., 'Nuclear weapons and East–West Relations', in Kaldor, M. and Smith, D. (eds), *Disarming Europe* (Merlin, London, 1982), p. 132. The latest version of this proposal is the Prague declaration by the Political Consultative Committee of the WTO, of 5 January 1983.

20 For example, Mearsheimer, J. J., 'Why the Soviets can't win quickly in Central Europe', *International Security*, Vol. 7, No. 1, Summer 1982, pp. 3-39.

21 'Keep a counter-punch', *The Economist*, Vol. 285, No. 7261, 30 October 1982, pp. 19-20.

22 Yost, D. S., 'Ballistic missile defence and the Atlantic Alliance', *International Security*, Vol. 7, No. 2, Fall 1982, pp. 143-74; Leitenberg, M., 'The neutron bomb—enhanced radiation warheads', *Journal of Strategic Studies*, Vol. 5, No. 3, September 1982, pp. 341-69 (on conventional substitutes for the neutron bomb); Bahr, E., 'Gemeinsame Sicherheit', *Europa-Archiv*, Vol. 37, No. 14, July 1982, pp. 421-30.

23 For example, Gouré, D. and McCormich, G., 'PGM: no panacea', in Alford (ed.)

(note 17), p. 111; Hoffman, S., 'NATO and nuclear weapons', *Foreign Affairs*, Vol. 60, No. 2, Winter 1981/82, p. 339.

24   Owen, D., 'Effective deterrence', in Barnaby, F. and Thomas, G. (eds), *The Nuclear Arms Race—Control or Catastrophe?* (Pinter, London, 1982), p. 40; Kaiser *et al.* (note 3), p. 363.

25   Compare the critical evaluation of the new technology by an East German author: Stöhr, R., 'Zu einigen gefährlichen waffentechnischen Entwicklungen in den imperialistischen Staaten', in Meissner, H. and Lohs, K-H. (eds.), *Wissenschaft und Frieden* (Akademie, Berlin, 1982), pp. 141f.

26   Stratmann (note 5), pp. 59–64.

27   Holst, J. J., 'Towards a New Political Order in Europe?', in Frei, D. (ed.), *Sicherheit durch Gleichgewicht?* (Schulthess, Zurich, 1982), pp. 84f.

28   Boserup, A., 'A strategy for peace and security', *Bulletin of Peace Proposals*, Vol. 12, No. 4, 1981, p. 406; Boserup, A., in Kaldor and Smith (eds) (note 19), pp. 185ff; Galtung, J., 'What kind of defence should we have?', in Myrdal, A. *et al.* (eds), *The Dynamics of European Nuclear Disarmament* (Spokesman, Nottingham, 1981), pp. 157ff; Galtung, J., 'NATO and the status of Western Europe', in Clarke, M. and Mowlam, M. (eds), *Debate on Disarmament* (Routledge & Kegan Paul, London, 1982), pp. 45ff; Boserup, A., 'Deterrence and defense', *Bulletin of the Atomic Scientists*, Vol. 37, No. 10, December 1981, p. 10; *Frieden mit anderen Waffen* (Rowohlt, Reinbek-Hamburg, 1981), pp. 164ff.

29   Aron, R., 'In search of security', *Trialogue*, No. 30/1, Summer/Fall 1982, pp. 7–13; Dean, J., 'Beyond first use', *Foreign Policy*, No. 48, Fall 1982, pp. 37ff; Palin, R. H., 'War in Europe: nuclear and conventional options', in Betts, R. K. (ed.), *Cruise Missiles* (Brookings, Washington, DC, 1981), pp. 173ff; Cordesman, A. H., 'Deterrence in the 1980s: Part I', *Adelphi Paper No. 175* (IISS, London, 1982), pp. 41f.

30   Speed (note 5), pp. 121–23; Holst, J. J., 'Deterrence and stability in the NATO–Warsaw Pact relationship', in O'Neill, R. and Horner, D. M. (eds), *New Directions in Strategic Thinking* (Allen & Unwin, London, 1981), chapter 6; Burrows and Edwards (note 5), chapter 8; Freedman, L., *Britain and Nuclear Weapons* (Macmillan, London, 1980), chapter 12; de Rose (note 9), p. 149; Neild, R., 'How to make up your mind about the bomb', *Bulletin of the Atomic Scientists*, Vol. 38, No. 1, January 1982, pp. 13–18.

31   Owen (note 24), p. 51.

32   Stratmann, K-P., 'Probleme der Bewertung militärischer Optionen der NATO und des Warschauer Paktes in Europa', in Forndran, E. and Friedrich, P. J. (eds), Rüstungskontrolle und Sicherheit in Europa (Europa-Union Verlag, Bonn, 1979), pp. 15–46; Hopmann, P. T., 'The "no first use" proposal and arms control initiatives in Europe', *Bulletin of Peace Proposals*, Vol. 13, No. 4, 1982, p. 273.

33   Holloway, D., 'Theatre nuclear weapons: the Soviet doctrine', in Kaldor and Smith (eds) (note 19), p. 102.

34   Dean (note 29), p. 51.

35   Alford, J., 'Confidence-building measures in Europe: the military aspects', in Bertram, C. (ed.), *Arms Control and Military Force* (Gower, London, 1980), p. 188; Holst, J. J. and Melander, K. A., 'European security and confidence-building measures', in Bertram, C. (ed.), pp. 233ff; Hopmann (note 32); Birnhaum, K. E., 'Confidence-building as an approach to cooperative arms regulations in Europe', in Huldt, B. and Lejins, A. (eds), *The Military Balance in Europe* (Swedish Institute of International Affairs, Stockholm, 1982), pp. 131ff.

Paper 4.   No-first-use of nuclear weapons

Shalheveth Freier
Research Fellow in the Department of Physics, Weizmann Institute of Science, Rehovot, Israel; former Chairman of the Israeli Atomic Energy Commission, 1971–76

The proposal has been extensively discussed that the nuclear weapon countries declare they will not be the first to use nuclear weapons if war breaks out and that they will dispose their armed forces in a manner which makes their declaration convincing and their dispositions verifiable. The authors of this proposal had in mind especially the confrontation in Europe of the military forces of the North Atlantic Treaty Organization and the Warsaw Treaty Organization. These forces are equipped by the USA and the USSR with nuclear weapons for battlefield or theatre use and backed up by the strategic carriers of the superpowers over intercontinental ranges. At the time of writing, the USSR has declared it will not be the first to use nuclear weapons in a war but only retaliate if attacked by such weapons. NATO, on the other hand, is officially committed to using nuclear weapons in order to fend off a Soviet invasion of western Europe, irrespective of the weapons employed by them.

A mere declaration on the part of the USSR naturally offers no reassurance, as nuclear weapons of varying range and improved performance are deployed against western Europe, but it sounds more forthcoming. The declared stance of NATO stems from an assessment that the conventional power of the WTO surpasses its own by an appreciable margin and that the USSR may be tempted to invade western Europe by way of FR Germany, if it can do so with impunity. NATO policy assumes that a first-use policy will deter the USSR, for an instant recourse to nuclear weapons threatens to set off nuclear exchanges which may eventually also embroil the strategic weapons of the USA and the USSR, wreaking such destruction as will leave hardly anyone to deplore the disparity between the original design and the ensuing calamity. If the 'first use' deterrent keeps war at bay, it may be justified; if it does not, the alternative would be disastrous for all involved. It is therefore perfectly legitimate to give the matter serious thought.

In this context, there are a few robust assumptions with which one has to live:

1. The nuclear arms race will go on, at least in development, as long as wars involving the interests of the major powers are conceivable, as they are at present. The most ominous aspects of this race concern the improvements of nuclear weapons in accuracy, capacity to penetrate and speedier summons into action, coupled with attempts to reduce the immunity of submarines—the erstwhile warrant of a second-strike capability. Through these developments, the risk of a pre-emptive recourse to nuclear weapons comes progressively nearer.

2. Of necessity, rigid concepts about the adversary—his designs, resolve and capacity—are built into military planning and procurement policies:

The USSR is deemed by NATO to have aggressive designs and not to be reluctant to invade western Europe, if it can do so. This assumption is based on its performance over the years, stretching from Berlin to Afghanistan, the suppression of secessionary moves in Czechoslovakia, Hungary and Poland, and interventions by proxy in Asia and Africa. Some argue that these precedents do not hold for western Europe, since the Soviet Union cannot rely on the loyal support of its allies in the WTO for an adventurous thrust to the west, while the nations so invaded might offer strong resistance in defence of their soil. Subversion might be a more promising and less risky way of furthering Soviet aims in western Europe. However much truth there might be in such speculations, they cannot possibly sway existing western military doctrines.

The Soviet perception is different. The Soviet view is that almost all destabilizing improvements in nuclear weaponry—and conventional weaponry for that matter—have been pioneered by the USA, just because its technology is better. The Soviet Union may well read malign intentions into these advances, though this interpretation is not borne out by US performance while it enjoyed nuclear superiority. Even assuming that the Soviet Union does not wish to further its cause in Europe by war, the Soviet military planner will not be content to base his development and procurement policy on an assumption of US restraint.

3. The USA must guarantee the inviolability of the eastern border of NATO—and especially of the FRG—and no allowance is made for a defence policy which would permit a Soviet advance, or for this advance to be absorbed, halted and eventually reversed. Such flexibility would cast doubt on the seriousness of the US engagement to the defence of Europe and on its resolve to stand up to Soviet challenges the world over. A war may be averted by such posture, but if it were to break out, it is more likely to reflect a pattern of changing fortunes than lead to mutual annihilation only on the border line of East and West.

4. The variety of proposals to restrain the development, production and deployment of nuclear weapons do not of course touch the core of the problem, a real or imagined readiness on the part of the superpowers and their allies to face each other in battle. But these proposals ('freezes' of all kinds, 'no use' declarations, SALT, START and the present discussions seeking to limit the deployment of intermediate range missiles) serve two purposes. First, they all help to create an atmosphere of sobriety in negotiations. Second, each individual proposal addresses itself to one particular aspect of the situation, such as forestalling a first strike by maintaining a credible second-strike capability.

From these four assumptions, let me try to evaluate the sense of a no-first-use pledge. It has two notably sound features, if some ancillary conditions are met. It says that even if war breaks out, the conflicting parties will wait awhile before they launch nuclear weapons. Such time for pause in actual conflict can be very important, because things do look different in actual situations from the way they are conceived in offices. Second, a no-first-use pledge is good only as long as the defence feels it can manage. Failing that, the nuclear arsenals and the threat of their eventual involvement are as real as before.

The first three assumptions (instant nuclear response with accurate and penetrating weapons with danger of escalation; the aggressive designs imputed to the USSR; the employment of nuclear weapons as soon as there is a Soviet crossing of the borders) tend to reduce the vital time for reflection before nuclear weapons are employed in an armed conflict. A no-first-use pledge and practice might thus afford a badly needed breathing space. With respect to the fourth assumption, a no-first-use pledge would be of the same order as all other prudential deeds and no more need to be said about this aspect of such a pledge.

However, there are ancillary conditions for a no-first-use pledge to be reliable, and if these conditions are met, a no-first-use practice is likely even in the absence of a pledge.

1. The conventional stance of the NATO Alliance should be such that in resolve, organization and material commitment, it would be able to face a Soviet challenge by conventional means in the first instance, in Europe and elsewhere.
2. NATO must be ready to allow for a conventional defence in depth, so that a sudden Soviet thrust—if it were to come—would not give the Soviet Union an overwhelming advantage.

As long as these conditions are not met, it is unlikely that a credible no-first-use pledge would be made. It is worthwhile, however, to build up the conventional capacity of NATO to the point where the threat of first use, or worse, its prompt implementation, dwindles in importance. The actual ravages of a nuclear war are really worse than those of conventional conflict.

All those in favour of the no-first-use pledge agree that it can realistically only be coupled with an improvement in NATO's conventional defences. Opinions differ as to whether NATO already has a conventional edge over the WTO—in means of warfare, manpower and motivation—or whether the draft would have to be reintroduced in the USA, NATO's forces would have to be better integrated, and the European allies would have to increase their military budgets in order to draw level with the Soviet Union. The proponents of no-first-use also make a detailed case for the character of NATO's defensive forces, the manner of their deployment and what precision-guided ammunition, cluster bombs and better control, command, communications and intelligence could do in order to blunt a Soviet advance or cut off its spearhead. In addition, it is claimed that the money spent on the very expensive logistics which go with the storage, transport and control of nuclear weapons for instant use, might be better spent on improvements in conventional defence. Other arguments in favour of a no-first-use pledge dwell on the inherent incredibility of an actual first use when the chips are down, with the destruction of what is supposed to be defended which would follow upon a first use and subsequent nuclear exchange. Lastly, there are those who maintain that the doctrine of a 'seamless linkage' is not at all convincing—a doctrine which commits the USA fully to the defence of Europe by way of exposing its mainland to Soviet nuclear attack through a first use of tactical nuclear weapons, escalating by way of intermediate range nuclear weapons to the US central strategic reserve at the extreme link of this chain.

The opponents of the no-first-use pledge maintain that it detracts from the stark deterrence for which it stands, that it is likely to weaken European trust in the USA and that no conceivable conventional effort can be mounted to match the nuclear deterrent. They say that the pledge is not verifiable; that the Soviet Union will use nuclear weapons—pledge or no pledge—and will profit from a Western renunciation of first use, which is the present major obstacle to their ambitions. Moreover, they maintain, US credibility may suffer world-wide if it changes its strategy.

The assessment in this paper is that a no-first-use proposal may be a good thing, if war breaks out, in order that there might be a little time to reflect before nuclear weapons enter the conflict; allowance must then indeed be made for an initial conventional phase, if war is to come. I do not think the deterrent effect of the nuclear arsenals is really impaired by such a no-first-use policy; however, I do think that the conventional stance and capacity of the USA and its allies requires a major refurbishing before a first-use doctrine could be dispensed with. But it is a goal worth striving for.

Paper 5.   The atom serves but one master

Pierre M. Gallois
French Air Force General (retd); Commercial Director of Société des Avions Marcel Dassault

Even before it became a nuclear power Mao Tse-tung's China announced that it would never be the first to use nuclear weapons. Such a commitment, even if not very seriously meant at the time, clearly involved no great risk. What other power would ever dare to take on, with conventional weapons, a thousand million people, even if they were equipped with nothing more formidable than rifles? The USSR, viewing the political kaleidoscope of western Europe and its feeble aggregate of national military contingents, could long ago have used similar language. It could indeed have addressed the United States—a democracy—in the same way. For it is hard to imagine that democracy blasting the Soviet Union with a nuclear attack.

In the world today, there co-exist two entirely different weapon systems, the nuclear and the conventional, the power of the former being such that—should circumstances permit its use—the latter would become entirely ineffective. A state enjoying military superiority (political homogeneity, a single command, more men under arms, more guns, aircraft and warships) runs no risk in announcing that it will never be the first to use nuclear weapons, since in a war fought with conventional arms the larger forces at its disposal will be ample for its defence. Conversely, the weaker side will be able to offset these military and political advantages only by immediate recourse to nuclear weapons; only by asserting a willingness to take this initiative in a crisis can a numerical superiority be offset and a potential aggressor deterred. Today, no other attitude on the part of the weaker side is likely to prove effective.

The proposal made by the Gang of Four—for so they call themselves: Messrs McGeorge Bundy, George Kennan, Robert McNamara and Gerard Smith—(reproduced here on pages 29–41) was accompanied by a recommendation they considered essential if their initiative was not to appear entirely senseless; namely, that the NATO countries, and especially those of western Europe, should step up their military expenditure, the money being spent on bigger and better conventional forces. Should it prove impossible to reverse the traditional Western inferiority in this respect, then a rough balance, the Four consider, should be the aim. Such a balance having been struck, the United States (the guaranteeing power) could then forgo its threat of using nuclear weapons first, so that, were western Europe to be invaded, the aggressor would be under no temptation to disarm the United States by a preventive nuclear strike against that country. Hence the supreme danger—a nuclear devastation of the United States—would be averted. And if battle were joined in Europe, the aggressor would soon be brought to a halt. He would then be in the most uncomfortable position of having either to retreat or to throw his nuclear forces into the fray. If he chose the latter course, the United States, still intact, would be able to launch a nuclear counter-strike with a clear conscience, not having been responsible for the escalation.

It should be clear enough, except perhaps to the Four themselves, that events would be most unlikely to obey this pattern. Many Americans, and especially those who favour no-first-use, still fail to grasp how great is the imbalance between East and West, even leaving nuclear forces out of the account. Indeed, in practically no sphere is there balance between the NATO countries and those of the WTO. In the East, an ambitious plan of social and political expansion has already been given effect, areas inhabited by more than a hundred million non-Russians having been occupied *manu militari* and subjected to the thrall of the Soviet Union. Far from the frontiers of this country, support is being given to revolutionary movements, while in Africa and Asia political systems pursuing ends at least complementary to those of Moscow hold sway over some four million square miles of territory. In the West, there has been a gradual retreat from former spheres of influence, a general willingness to settle for a bird in the hand rather than a bird in the bush, and a disinclination to take risks. Again, in the East there has been a remarkable degree of stability in the direction of affairs. Between 1917 and 1982 the Soviet Union has been successively governed by no more than five men. In the West, there has been a whole series of heads of state and of governments, all with their own ideas of the national interest, and with neither the means nor, above all, the terms of office required to attain their ends. In this respect, France, with more than 60 governments during this period, carries the contrast with the Soviet Union to almost grotesque extremes.

In the East, there has been the same continuity in the high command as in government. Admiral Gorchkov has been in charge of the Soviet Navy for no less than 26 years, while Mr Gromyko, in the course of a lengthy career, has had to deal with more than 100 ministers for foreign affairs of the Atlantic Alliance countries. A marked contrast to the position in the West, where the rules governing promotion, combined with the vagaries of political fortune, mean that nobody can look forward to more than a brief period in high office.

In the East, governments do not find their hands tied by public opinion, which does not count, whereas in the West politicians are above all concerned with their popularity ratings and the press will publish anything likely to boost sales, even though the national interest may suffer as a result.

Similar imbalances exist in military affairs. In the East a huge expanse of land, much of it thinly populated, means that, for instance, mobile missile-launchers can be readily deployed. In the West the industrial countries of western Europe are populated by swarming millions, and governments cannot afford to overlook public opinion. If Messrs Schmidt and Carter had so much as given a thought to this kind of imbalance, they would never have attempted to counter SS-20 missiles with the Pershing II.

Moreover, the East has at its disposal huge masses of men who can be readily mobilized and kept for long periods under arms at little cost. The Soviet soldier has to make do on less than 10 dollars a month. What market-economy country could man its frontiers if its sons were paid with similar parsimony? This, a truly basic imbalance, seems to have escaped the Four.

Nor have the Four given much thought to the military consequences of their proposals, which would have momentous implications for the European allies of the United States.

1. An announcement by Washington that it would never use nuclear weapons to stop an attack launched by the conventional forces of the WTO would enormously simplify the task of the Soviet Commander-in-Chief. He would know in advance that he was free to concentrate his forces, rather than having to disperse them to minimize the threat from US nuclear weapons. He would be virtually invited to make full use of his superior numbers so as to bring a superior weight of fire to bear at a point or points of his choosing. The Four may perhaps be unaware that the effectiveness of conventional forces is directly proportional to their degree of concentration and to the weight of metal they can launch on a target.

2. The Four seem to have forgotten that the initiative in launching a conflict in Europe can come only from the East. Recent history shows that whenever the Soviet regular forces intervene (as in Hungary, Czechoslovakia and Afghanistan), there is no subsequent withdrawal. The Soviet Army built the Soviet empire and holds it together; any evident failure on its part would be fraught with the threat of disintegration. It follows that if Soviet forces were committed in Europe, they would set out to win at all costs, using every weapon, even the most destructive. The doctrine of no-first-use means reliance on a conventional counterstroke which clearly will not deter. Furthermore, with the adoption of this doctrine, the initiative and hence the choice of surprise tactics which it confers would pass to the Soviet Commander-in-Chief. Western forces having been rendered vulnerable, he would be free to use his abundant manpower and resources to destroy them by conventional and nuclear means.

3. The western European countries are living under a military threat which is not the same for all of them at any one time. It would indeed make better sense for the WTO countries to adopt a 'salami strategy', that is, a policy of piecemeal gains. But armed with conventional weapons only, what could individual European countries do to halt the armed hordes converging on them?

4. Hitherto, the defence of western Europe has been based on a dual system whereby the western Europeans supply a conventional contribution to the common defence while the USA brandishes the awesome threat of nuclear intervention. It now seems that Americans—and Americans of some standing at that—are prepared to denounce the arrangement, and this at a time when the US

government has been feverishly trying to push its allies into signing a non-proliferation treaty, thus making them dependent on a US nuclear guarantee!

5. In the United States, it is already being insinuated that the US Expeditionary Force in western Europe is no longer safe. Adoption of no-first-use would make its uselessness plain for all to see, and the way would be open for the US Supreme Command to call for repatriation of US forces—a development no doubt tacitly desired by the Four. Moreover, if no-first-use were to be officially adopted as a principle underlying western European defence strategy, certain practical consequences would ensue, namely:

Stocks of US nuclear warheads, bombs and shells would have to be shipped back home, for it is hard to imagine the US government leaving such a massive potential for destruction at the mercy of some rapid thrust by the conventional forces of the WTO. There would be no more US nuclear weapons in western Europe, which would cease to be a trip-wire for their use; only if the USA itself were attacked would they come into play. In such circumstances, the Europeans, with their conventional forces, would be at the mercy of the conventional and nuclear forces of the WTO.

If the US Expeditionary Force were nevertheless to remain in Europe, it would become just another national contingent, neither more nor less formidable than any other. In such circumstances, supreme command would probably devolve upon a German officer, FR Germany being the major contributor to the collective defence effort.

It is doubtful whether the Four are naive enough to be unmindful of the political consequences of their proposals. The aim they are pursuing in 1982 is a return to the ideas prevalent in the Kennedy Administration, 20 years ago, as regards the security of the European allies. The idea at that time was to keep the latter within the US sphere of influence, but without excessive risk, and without provoking a powerful Soviet Union. Withdrawal of nuclear weapons from forward areas, the doctrine of the graduated response, the idea of a 'pause for reflection'—all these were designed exclusively to reduce the risks of the commitments entered into when NATO was set up. Now, when the USSR has attained military superiority in every sphere, Messrs Bundy, Kennan, McNamara and Smith seem to believe that no-first-use will secure their country's disengagement, while reducing the importance of western Europe to that of any other potential battlefield not protected by nuclear weapons. It may not be amiss to point out that in some of the areas thus 'denuclearized', conventional warfare is being ferociously waged.

In all probability adoption of no-first-use would have dire effects on the military organization of the NATO Alliance. The fundamental balance between conventional and nuclear arms would disappear and NATO would fade into insignificance. Already, because of the increasing military might of the USSR (and because the allies themselves have made mistakes with regard to enhanced-radiation weapons and the deployment of Pershing IIs and cruise missiles in Europe), the military organization of the Alliance is in some disarray. Were their counsels heeded, the Four would be dealing it a death blow.

They would have proved that (as was indeed felt in certain quarters in France after Hiroshima) no military alliance based on the use of nuclear weapons can be lasting. Nuclear weapons, it would seem, only ensure the survival of the countries possessing them.

Such a conviction could not but encourage nuclear proliferation, each country looking to its own defence in awareness of the fact that conventionally-armed forces are powerless against nuclear weapons.

Recent spectacular increases in the accuracy of long-range weapons (self-steering pilotless aircraft, such as cruise missiles) are an additional incitement to rely on nuclear arms. Thus, the countries bordering on the USSR are well aware that, should Moscow so decide, they would be threatened by the SS-20, especially in its later, more accurate versions. The governments concerned are gradually coming round to the realization that their own conventional forces could be paralysed by no more than a handful of nuclear projectiles. Hence some of them are thinking of acquiring their own nuclear arms, which are easier to protect against attack than military units of the traditional kind. Nuclear weapon-free zones, or areas devoid of military installations of any kind, can prove attractive only to those who reason with an eye to the past. The range, speed and accuracy of existing weapons are such that the nuclear weapon-free zone can be of no military significance, even though the idea may hold a superficial attraction for public opinion.

As we have seen, the Four have made proposals the implications of which go well beyond the present predicament of western Europe. These proposals have at least one merit—they show that weapons of mass destruction cannot be supranational. They can be expected only to defend the vital interests of the state possessing them.

Paper 6. No-first-use—a first step in eliminating nuclear weapons

Alfonso García Robles

Representative of Mexico to the Conference on Disarmament, Geneva; Nobel Laureate for Peace, 1982

Robert Oppenheimer, as he watched the first test of the atomic bomb, is said to have seen in his mind's eye the awesome effects of future nuclear weapons, recalling the Hindu words: "I am become Death, Shatterer of Worlds."[1]

A similar thought is expressed in the Pastoral Letter prepared for the National Conference of the Catholic Bishops of the United States by its Committee on War and Peace, which was approved on 3 May 1983. In this document one can read *inter alia*:

In the nuclear arsenals of the United States or the Soviet Union alone, there exists a capacity to do something no other age could imagine: We can threaten the entire planet... Today the destructive potential of the nuclear powers threatens the human person, the civilization we have slowly constructed and even the created order itself...

Today the possibilities for placing political and moral limits on nuclear war are so minimal that the moral task, like the medical, is prevention: As a people, we must refuse to legitimate the idea of nuclear war...

The chances of keeping use limited seem remote, and the consequences of escalation to mass destruction would be appalling.... the danger of escalation is so great that it would be morally unjustifiable to initiate nuclear war in any form.... We find the moral responsibility of beginning nuclear war not justified by rational political objectives...

This judgement affirms that the willingness to initiate nuclear war entails a distinct, weighty moral responsibility; it involves transgressing a fragile barrier—political, psychological and moral—which has been constructed since 1945... we judge resort to nuclear weapons to counter a conventional attack to be morally unjustifiable.[2]

Dozens of analogous statements coming from the most authoritative sources could be easily quoted to substantiate these views. Albert Einstein and Bertrand Russell, in the historic Manifesto which they issued in 1955 and which gave birth to the Pugwash Movement, declared emphatically:

We have to learn to think in a new way. We have to learn to ask ourselves, not what steps can be taken to give military victory to whatever group we prefer, for there no longer are such steps; the question we have to ask ourselves is: what steps can be taken to prevent a military contest of which the issue must be disastrous to all parties?...

It is feared that if many H-bombs are used there will be universal death—sudden only for a minority, but for the majority a slow torture of disease and disintegration . . .

Here, then, is the problem which we present to you, stark and dreadful and inescapable: Shall we put an end to the human race; or shall mankind renounce war? . . .[3]

To fully understand the validity and irrefutable justification of those appraisals, it would be enough to ponder briefly on the following statistics:

The atomic bomb which destroyed Hiroshima in 1945 was a 12.5 kiloton bomb. At present nuclear weapons of 20 megatons, that is, of a destructive capacity 1 600 times greater, are nothing extraordinary.

The destructive capacity of the nuclear arsenals of the two superpowers—the Soviet Union and the United States—alone is, according to the most conservative estimates, well above one million Hiroshima bombs, enough to kill the entire population of the Earth many times over.

It is, therefore, easy to understand why the General Assembly of the United Nations, the most representative organ of the world community, was able to approve by consensus in 1978, at its first special session devoted to disarmament, a Final Document in which the Assembly:

expressed its alarm at "the threat to the very survival of mankind posed by the existence of nuclear weapons and the continuing arms race";

called attention to the fact that "Mankind today is confronted with an unprecedented threat of self-extinction arising from the massive and competitive accumulation of the most destructive weapons ever produced. Existing arsenals of nuclear weapons alone are more than sufficient to destroy all life on earth";

underlined that "The increase in weapons, especially nuclear weapons, far from helping to strengthen international security, on the contrary weakens it";

stressed that "Enduring international peace and security cannot be built on the accumulation of weaponry by military alliances nor be sustained by a precarious balance of deterrence or doctrines of strategic superiority";

declared that "All the peoples of the world have a vital interest in the success of disarmament negotiations";

and emphasized that "While the final objective of the efforts of all States should continue to be general and complete disarmament under effective international control, the immediate goal is that of the elimination of the danger of a nuclear war".[4]

As a corollary to those declarations, the Assembly proclaimed the following conclusion: "Nuclear weapons pose the greatest danger to mankind and to the survival of civilization. It is essential to halt and reverse the nuclear arms race in all its aspects in order to avert the danger of war involving nuclear weapons. The ultimate goal in this context is the complete elimination of nuclear weapons."[4]

It is obvious that reaching this "ultimate goal" will require considerable time and effort. The achievement of nuclear disarmament will need, as the Final Document itself clearly stated in its paragraphs 49 and 50, a complex process which "should be carried out in such a way, and requires measures to ensure, that the security of all States is guaranteed at progressively lower levels of nuclear armaments . . .". Such a process will have to include the urgent negotiation of agreements at appropriate stages and with adequate measures of verification satisfactory to the states concerned for achieving the cessation of the qualitative improvement and development of nuclear-weapon systems; the cessation of the production of all types of nuclear weapon and their means of delivery, and of the production of fissionable material for weapon purposes, and the adoption of "a comprehensive, phased programme with agreed time-frames, whenever feasible, for progressive and balanced reduction of stockpiles of nuclear weapons and their means of delivery, leading to their ultimate and complete elimination at the earliest possible time".[5]

In the long road which needs to be covered in order to reach the goal of the total elimination of nuclear weapons, a commitment to no-first-use of such dreadful instruments of mass destruction represents a progress of the utmost significance. If such a commitment, which has already been solemnly and unilaterally proclaimed by China and the Soviet Union, were to be undertaken as well by the other three states which possess nuclear weapons, the result would be, from a moral, psychological and pragmatic point of view, the same as if the five powers in question had become parties to a treaty forbidding the first use of nuclear weapons.

Since so far it is only in the United States, and in Europe within the Atlantic Alliance framework, where the first use of nuclear weapons has been seriously considered as a desirable proposition, it is encouraging to note that in recent months many prominent personalities of great prestige on international matters have either favourably examined whether, or definitely proposed that, the United States and the other members of the NATO Alliance should abandon their strategy based on the first use of nuclear weapons. Inasmuch as they are quite numerous, the few examples quoted below should merely be taken as the result of a strict illustrative selection. The most notable example is that of the four US high officials of well established reputation, McGeorge Bundy, George F. Kennan, Robert S. McNamara and Gerard Smith, whose article is reprinted on pages 29–41.

Egon Bahr, Chairman of the Subcommittee on Arms Control and Disarmament of the Bundestag of FR Germany, referred to the suggestions made by these four Americans in the following terms:

The 'no-first-use' proposal by the four Americans known as reliable proponents of Atlantic mutual security would, if adopted, have immense political implications: The discussion that so burdens the alliance—the European suspicion that America could be tempted, in the event of an incident, to wage a nuclear war limited to Europe—would be finished. A one-sided no-first-use doctrine by NATO would thus strengthen the alliance politically and increase the feeling of security in Europe.[5]

If Mr Bahr appeared in this article, written in May 1982, to be strongly in favour of a "one sided no-first-use doctrine by NATO", he certainly must be now even more inclined to support such a doctrine since the Soviet Union, on 15 June of the same year, solemnly announced at the United Nations General

Assembly that it will never be the first to use nuclear weapons.

Paul C. Warnke, former Director of the United States Arms Control and Disarmament Agency, stated:

To say that we must stick with a 'first use' option is to say that we cannot do without nuclear weapons, that we are safer because they were invented, that even if we could rid the world of them this would be a bad idea. But I for one cannot join the nuclear weapons cheering section. And I believe the American public will be shocked and dismayed when they understand the implications of a policy that we might ever start a nuclear war . . .

It should be made very clear that any first use of nuclear arms by the other side will invite and receive instant nuclear retaliation. But it should be made just as clear that the Soviet Union and its people will remain safe from our nuclear weapons unless, and only unless, their's are used against us or our allies. In such a policy, and only in such a policy, lies genuine security.[6]

Jonathan Dean, who was Ambassador in charge of the US Delegation to the Mutual and Balanced Force Reduction talks from 1978 to 1981, wrote:

The debate over the first use strategy is only one aspect of an underlying problem of NATO strategy—continued primary reliance on the American extended deterrent at a time when the United States has lost its nuclear superiority over the Soviet Union . . . . Attempts to do so primarily by improving NATO's nuclear arsenal in Western Europe do not have the right emphasis. They elicit controversy and compound the problem. The conclusion seems clear: The changed U.S.–Soviet nuclear relationship necessitates a change in NATO strategy, a shift away from primary reliance on nuclear deterrence to primary deterrence by conventional forces.[7]

John Newhouse, author of one of the most revealing books on the bilateral negotiations known as SALT I, has published an article in which he reproduces what was said to him by some prominent public figures about the question of no-first-use of nuclear weapons:

The former Secretary of State Cyrus Vance is quoted as having stated:
'I agree in principle with the idea of no first use, but feel we should adopt it only after negotiations that have created parity in conventional forces in Europe . . . . We are stronger conventionally than we concede, although there is some disparity. I agree with the view that the Europeans tend to exaggerate the weakness of the conventional balance because of their reluctance to yield the nuclear option.'[8]

The views of George Ball, a former Under-Secretary of State of whom Mr Newhouse says that he "has probably had as much involvement with Europe's security and its politics as any other living American", are reported to be the following:

I'm very glad my four friends have pushed this into the public domain, and I wish it had happened sooner. We must move away from the self-deception that a battlefield nuclear weapon might be used to avoid NATO forces' being overrun. Using it would create the very strong possibility of a general nuclear war. It lacks credibility and doesn't make any sense . . . Clinging to this doctrine means—or seems to mean—that we regard these weapons as war-fighting weapons. They aren't. We can go only so long indulging in fantasies.[8]

The group entitled "Generals for Peace and Disarmament"—which comprises a Marshal, a former President of Portugal, ten retired Generals and an Admiral, also retired, all of them nationals of member countries of NATO, within which they performed a large variety of important military duties (including in one case that of Deputy of the NATO Supreme Commander of Europe for Nuclear Planning)—submitted to the delegations of the United Nations Second Special Session on Disarmament a Memorandum in which they stated *inter alia*:

Nuclear weapons are not suitable for pursuing political aims; their employment involves the risk of self extinction; it is highly unlikely in the extreme that their use could be limited to specific regions of the world or to specific target systems; there will therefore be no winner in a nuclear war; the loser will be mankind as a whole . . . .

Defense policy is only useful if it serves national security interests . . . . Anyone who bases his defense on a first-use strategy is contemplating his suicide . . . . We give highest priority to a declared renunciation of all kinds of nuclear warfare.[9]

The Pontifical Academy of Sciences, which comprises 70 members from many different countries, and with the participation of representatives of 35 Academies of Sciences of the world, West and East, approved in September 1982, after two successive meetings held in London and Rome in March and June of the same year, a declaration which, *inter alia*, states:

The existing arsenals, if employed in a major war, could result in the immediate deaths of many hundreds of millions of people, and of untold millions more later through a variety of after-effects. For the first time, it is possible to cause damage on such a catastrophic scale as to wipe out a large part of civilization and to endanger its very survival . . . .

Science can offer the world no real defense against the consequences of nuclear war . . . .

The catastrophe of nuclear war can and must be prevented. Leaders and governments have a grave responsibility to fulfill in this regard. But it is humankind as a whole which must act for its survival. This is the greatest moral issue that humanity has ever faced, and there is no time to be lost . . . .

II. In view of these threats of global nuclear catastrophe, we declare:

—Nuclear weapons are fundamentally different from conventional weapons. They must not be regarded as acceptable instruments of warfare. Nuclear warfare would be a crime against humanity . . . .

—The current arms race increases the risk of nuclear war. The race must be stopped, the development of new more destructive weapons must be curbed, and nuclear forces must be reduced, with the ultimate goal of complete nuclear disarmament. The sole purpose of nuclear weapons, as long as they exist, must be to deter nuclear war . . . .

. . . .we call upon all nations:

—Never to be the first to use nuclear weapons . . .[10]

At the United Nations Second Special Session on Disarmament in June 1982, the representatives of 42 member states referred, in the general debate, to no-first-use. The relevant statements are set out in appendix III, page 133. Of those representatives, 35—that is, almost 90 per cent—expressed themselves strongly in favour of no-first-use, while four were somewhat ambiguous in their pronouncements and only three made declarations contrary to it.

The United Nations General Assembly has unanimously declared that the elimination of the danger of a nuclear war is "the most acute and urgent task of the present day".[4] There is an obvious, essential and axiomatic difference between nuclear and conventional weapons, a difference which some states—fortunately a very small number, indeed—do not yet seem willing to comprehend. It is not possible to pretend that a no-first-use commitment has no value in the belief that such promises can never be dependable amid the stresses of war. Were we to accept such a thesis, we would be burying international law itself since what would apply to the commitments would also be applicable to any treaty or convention, be it bilateral or multilateral.

Finally, it is morally and politically inadmissible that the survival of mankind should be made hostage to the peculiar perceptions of security of a few states. Pending the achievement of the total elimination of nuclear weapons, as agreed by consensus at UNSSOD I, the least the peoples of the world are entitled to expect from all the nuclear weapon states, as a tangible first step towards that goal, is a firm commitment, like the one already undertaken by China and the Soviet Union, to no-first-use of nuclear weapons.

References
1 *Bhagavadgita*, chapter 11, verse 32.
2 *The Pastoral Letter on War and Peace, The Challenge of Peace: God's Promise and Our Response*, Origins (NC Documentary Service, Washington, D.C.), Vol. 1, No. 1, 19 May 1983, pp. 13, 15.
3 *The Russell-Einstein Manifesto*, delivered at a press conference in London, 9 July 1955.
4 UN Document A/Res/S-10/2, 13 July 1978.
5 Bahr, E., *New York Times*, 10 May 1982.
6 Warnke, P. C., speech delivered to the National Press Club, Washington, DC, 14 April 1982.
7 Dean, J., 'Beyond first use', *Foreign Policy*, No. 48, Fall 1982, p. 52.
8 Newhouse, J., 'Arms and orthodoxy', *The New Yorker*, 7 June 1982, pp. 96–97.
9 Memorandum to UNSSOD II by "Generals for peace and disarmament".
10 *Declaration on Prevention of Nuclear War*, by an assembly of Presidents of Scientific Academies and other scientists from all over the world, convened by the Pontifical Academy of Science, 23–24 September 1982 (Vatican 82).

Paper 7. Views on a commitment to no-first-use of nuclear weapons

Cai Mengsun

Former Director of the Institute for International Strategic Studies, Beijing, People's Republic of China; now Military, Naval and Air Attaché of the People's Republic of China in Canada

Over the past two years the two superpowers, the United States and the Soviet Union, have been engaged in a new round of a more intensified nuclear arms race, whose object is to improve the quality of their respective nuclear weapons. As a result, the deployment of nuclear weapons is now more widespread and the stockpile of nuclear warheads is higher than ever. The danger of a nuclear war is looming larger. At the same time, however, anti-nuclear war movements have gained momentum all over the world. In Europe and Asia, as well as in the United States, the new anti-nuclear mass movements have been attacking the nuclear arms race between the United States and the Soviet Union; they have played a significant role in forcing these two superpowers to sit down and hold negotiations on nuclear disarmament. Thus the present situation is both more dangerous and more hopeful.

In current anti-nuclear movements, many good ideas and proposals have been put forward on nuclear disarmament, such as the establishment of nuclear weapon-free zones, the limitation and reduction of nuclear stockpiles, and the commitment by all nuclear powers to no-first-use of nuclear weapons, and so on. Today, conditions have never been so propitious for reaching an international agreement on no-first-use of nuclear weapons. As a necessary first step towards eliminating the danger of a nuclear war, all the nuclear powers, especially the United States and the Soviet Union, should undertake a commitment to no-first-use of nuclear weapons, as a prelude to the realization of the ultimate goal of prohibiting and destroying them. The government of the People's Republic of China has always had a positive stand on this issue. From the very beginning of its possession of nuclear weapons, China has time and again declared that the purpose of China's development of nuclear weapons is to break the nuclear monopoly of the two superpowers, to defend itself against aggression, and finally to eliminate nuclear weapons. The government has pledged to the world that at no time and under no circumstances will China be the first to use nuclear weapons. China has also committed itself never to use or threaten to use nuclear weapons against non-nuclear states. It is because it considers it has a duty to help prevent nuclear wars and preserve world peace that China has undertaken these obligations unconditionally and unilaterally. But it is a matter of regret that China's stand for a long time did not meet with any positive response from the United States or the Soviet Union.

In recent years, the Soviet Union has somewhat changed its attitude towards this question, after having maintained and enhanced its superiority in conventional forces over Western countries. It took over China's initiatives on no-first-use of nuclear weapons as if it were its own and tried to outmanoeuvre and embarrass the United States, but refused to undertake the obligations unilaterally. Only in June 1982 was a formal declaration made at the UN Second Special Session on Disarmament that the Soviet Union would assume unilaterally an obligation not to be the first to use nuclear weapons.

This is progress on the part of the Soviet Union. However, the Soviet declaration is essentially different from the Chinese statement. The most important difference is that the Soviet commitment to no-first-use of nuclear weapons is not unconditional. In its declaration, it emphasizes the importance of how the other nuclear powers act and whether or not they follow the Soviet example. It leaves an impression that if the other nuclear powers do not follow suit, the Soviet Union could break its promise at any moment.

Besides, the Soviet declaration does not say a single word about the obligation not to use or threaten to use nuclear weapons against non-nuclear states. It implies that the Soviet Union still wants to levy nuclear blackmail on them. These differences lessen the value of the Soviet declaration in the eyes of the international community.

There are various comments on the real motive behind the Soviet declaration. Most observers regard it as a propaganda gesture catering to a world-wide abhorrence of nuclear war and aimed to win over world public opinion—especially that of the anti-nuclear movements in the United States and western European countries. In so doing, the Soviet Union hopes to put the United States in a negative position, to sow discord between the United States and its European allies, and finally to strengthen the Soviet strategic posture backed by its superior conventional forces. Judging from past Soviet behaviour, and from its military doctrines, which always attach great importance to the use of nuclear weapons, and in the light of the fact that shortly after its declaration of no-first-use of nuclear weapons at the UN General Assembly the Soviet Union staged a ballistic missile launching manoeuvre, it is quite natural for people to think that this view is well founded. Therefore, while extending a welcome to the Soviet declaration, one must keep an eye on Soviet performance and guard against being deceived.

As for the United States, it has up to now refused to commit itself not to be the first to use nuclear weapons, especially tactical nuclear weapons. The United States has considered the possible use of tactical nuclear weapons as a last resort to deter Soviet conventional aggression against western Europe. It fears that with a commitment to no-first-use its nuclear force would no longer be an effective deterrent.

However, in view of its immense destructive power, an invulnerable nuclear force could to a certain degree play a deterrent role in preventing a new world war, particularly a nuclear war. The very presence of nuclear weapons would make any potential aggressor hesitate to launch large-scale aggressive war. It has to take into account the opponent's destructive retaliation.

Because of their immense destructive power, nuclear weapons might be of very limited actual use in a future war. In fact, no one can rely on the employment of nuclear weapons to win a war. Under the nuclear balance of terror between the two superpowers, neither strategic nor tactical nuclear weapons could be used without resulting in massive mutual destruction. In this sense, it is unrealistic to base the credibility of deterrence on the use of tactical nuclear weapons, or to envisage them as a last resort to contain Soviet conventional aggression against western Europe. If the Soviet Union waged a conventional war against western Europe, it is open to doubt whether the United States would decide to use nuclear weapons to protect western Europe at the risk of inviting Soviet strategic nuclear strikes at US territory. Even if the United States were to decide to use nuclear weapons and were to succeed in limiting the nuclear battlefield to Europe, the European countries would be destroyed completely, no matter which side won the war. This horrible prospect makes the idea of a tactical or theatre nuclear war unacceptable to European countries.

It seems that the best way of preserving European security is to rely not on first use of nuclear weapons, but on strengthening Europe's conventional defensive forces in proportion to the Soviet military buildup and the threat it poses. In the light of NATO's tremendous war potential, including its armed forces, economic power, military technologies and manpower resources, there is no reason to believe that NATO would be unable to defend itself with conventional forces against Soviet conventional aggression. It is harmful to confidence to over-estimate the power of Soviet conventional forces.

The conclusion is that it is not realistic to think of the first use of nuclear weapons as a counter to a superior conventional offensive; the arguments of the United States for not committing itself to no-first-use of nuclear weapons are therefore untenable.

To protect mankind from a nuclear holocaust, it is urgent to demand that all the nuclear powers, especially the United States, take a positive approach in this regard and undertake an obligation not to be the first to use nuclear weapons. A commitment to no-first-use of nuclear weapons by all the nuclear powers would at least ease international tension and create a favourable climate for nuclear disarmament talks, though it is far from enough to diminish the menace of a nuclear war and eliminate the threat to non-nuclear states.

The commitment to no-first-use of nuclear weapons does not affect either nuclear power's possession of large stockpiles of nuclear weapons; nor does it prevent them from continuing a nuclear arms race, with the emphasis on upgrading quality. In the nuclear age, the possible use of nuclear weapons in the case of grave conflicts and crises cannot be precluded merely because the nuclear powers undertake not to be the first to use nuclear weapons. And in reality one can never be assured that the agreement will not be violated by powers seeking world hegemony through aggression and adventure. Mr Gromyko asserted in his statement to the UN Second Special Session on Disarmament that if the other nuclear powers follow the Soviet example not to be the first to use nuclear weapons, "the likelihood of an outbreak of nuclear war will in fact be reduced to zero".[1] This assertion is arbitrary if it has no ulterior motives.

The more effective way to prevent the danger of a nuclear war and eliminate nuclear threats to non-nuclear weapon states is to reach an agreement by all the nuclear weapon states not only to pledge not to be the first to use nuclear weapons, but also to take other essential measures, as follows:

First, the United States and the Soviet Union, who have the largest nuclear arsenals, should stop nuclear tests, stop development and production of nuclear weapons and substantially cut back all types of nuclear weapon and means of delivery. After that, all the nuclear powers, including Great Britain, China and France, should commit themselves to halting the development and manufacture of nuclear weapons, and proceed to reduce nuclear weapon stocks until all nuclear weapons are destroyed.

Second, conventional disarmament should begin simultaneously with nuclear disarmament. Since the end of World War II, all wars have been fought with conventional arms. The superpowers often use their conventional forces as a means of aggression and expansion. And a large-scale conventional war in any densely populated area would not be much less destructive than a nuclear war. Furthermore, in the nuclear age a conventional war always has the risk that it might escalate into nuclear war; indeed it is the most likely ladder leading to a nuclear war. If people are preoccupied only with preventing nuclear war and relax their vigilance against a conventional one, the possibility of the outbreak of nuclear war may still be left open. Therefore, in order to prevent nuclear war, people must exert the same efforts to prevent a conventional one as well. All states in the world, the United States and the Soviet Union in particular, should assume the obligation not to use conventional armaments for intervention or aggression against any other country. They should also reduce conventional armaments through various arms control and disarmament negotiations to the lowest level required by the basic necessity of defending their own security, so as to make any military intervention and aggression impossible.

To sum up, under the present international situation a commitment to no-first-use of nuclear weapons by all the nuclear powers would be a positive step. Efforts should be made to conclude an agreement to this effect. However, people should not rest content with this objective alone. Today, the harsh reality is that the two superpowers, the United States and the Soviet Union, are vigorously pursuing hegemonist policies. While paying lip service to nuclear as well as conventional disarmament, both of them stop short of any practical action. The UN Second Special Session on Disarmament ended in failure because of their obstruction and sabotage. All this has proved that there do exist dangers of war, including nuclear war. The peoples of the world have a long way to go in their struggle against nuclear war and to preserve world peace.

Reference

[1] UN document A/S-12/PV.12, 15 June 1982, pp. 28–30.

Paper 8. On the question of non-resort to the first use of nuclear weapons

Mikhail A. Milshtein
Head of Section, Institute of US and Canadian Studies, Academy of Sciences of the USSR

I. Introduction

A paradoxical, delicate and dangerous situation is developing in the world at the present time. On the one hand, it is generally recognized that a nuclear war, even if there had been an attempt to restrict it to a particular territory, target or number of strikes, would inevitably develop into a general, all-out war, with catastrophic consequences for the world.

Virtually all authorities agree that a nuclear war, once unleashed, could destroy human civilization and, possibly, life itself. There would be no winner in such a war, and the survivors would probably envy the dead.

On the other hand, in spite of this general realization, the nuclear arms race is not only continuing, but is gathering fresh momentum as new, more sophisticated, destructive and lethal means of mass annihilation are added to the arsenals of the nuclear states. This ominous 'progress' in the further sophistication of nuclear weapons and the means of their delivery has now reached a dangerous point.

II. Proliferation and stockpiling of nuclear weapons

Let us begin with the proliferation of nuclear weapons. In 1945, the United States was the only country possessing nuclear weapons. Scientists and specialists were of the view that a long time would elapse before another country could unravel the secrets of nuclear weapons and acquire a potential for their production and deployment. As is often the case, the scientists and specialists seriously miscalculated. Since then, the number of nuclear powers has increased from one to five. The secret of developing nuclear weapons is a secret no longer; the industrial capabilities for building such weapons are now available not only to the nuclear powers, but also to several more countries. According to US intelligence data, by the year 2000 there will be 31 states capable of producing their own nuclear

111

weapons.[1] Thus, proliferation of nuclear weapons may become inevitable. Further, together with these growing capabilities for the production of nuclear weapons, pockets of tension and conflict situations are also proliferating in the world—in the Middle East, in the South Atlantic, in the south of Africa, in Iran and Iraq, and elsewhere. If proliferation of nuclear weapons is not halted for good in the future, any such conflict might rapidly spill over into a general conflagration.

Consider the process of stockpiling nuclear warheads and the means of their delivery. In 1945, the USA possessed only a few atomic bombs. At present, according to SIPRI estimates, about 50 000 nuclear warheads exist in the world. This means that during the 38 years since the first use of nuclear weapons by the United States against the Japanese cities of Hiroshima and Nagasaki the nuclear powers have added to their arsenals an average of about 1 400 nuclear warheads a year, or four nuclear warheads a day. At present, there are 3–7 tonnes equivalent of TNT for each inhabitant of the Earth. The quantity as well as the variety of the means of delivery have also increased immeasurably. Far from declining, the process continues to gather momentum. According to US press reports, if the MX missile and Trident programmes are fulfilled on time, the United States would increase its arsenal of strategic nuclear warheads alone to 20 000. If one assumes that these weapons (the MX missile and Trident II) are deployed some time in the second half of the 1980s, then the quantity of strategic nuclear ammunition will be growing at a rate of about 2 000 warheads a year, or 5–6 warheads a day. And this is only strategic weapons. To this one must add that the USA no longer possesses nuclear superiority; this development was bound to happen. A rough parity has been achieved between the USA and the USSR in the nuclear field, and neither country will allow the other to upset this parity. This creates a superabundance of nuclear weapons. When there are too many weapons, strategists and politicians start hectically looking for ways in which to use the 'surplus'. This means looking at the possibility of waging a nuclear war, 'winning' such a war, or making such a war 'limited' or 'safe' for the side unleashing it.

Qualitative developments

'Progress' in the development of nuclear weapons is not, however, confined to a quantitative buildup of the warheads and the means of delivery. The process of qualitative sophistication of nuclear weapons is even more formidable. The avenues for qualitative improvement of lethal weapons are manifold: they include improving delivery means, reducing the weight of nuclear warheads, developing nuclear mini-weapons, adding, on US initiative, neutron weapons to NATO arsenals in the near future, increasing the number of targetable re-entry vehicles in strategic missiles and substantially improving their accuracy. 'Waiting in the wings' are new systems of weapons, which will add to the fears that one side might acquire the capacity for a first, crippling strike; such developments will increasingly undermine international stability. Also 'waiting in the wings' are weapons which it will be extremely difficult or well-nigh impossible to control—either by national or any other technical means. And if international control collapses, this will inevitably bring down with it the whole process of negotiation and agreement on arms limitations, thus adding to suspicion, fear and uncertainty.

George Kennan, former US ambassador to the Soviet Union and a well-known US public figure, wrote that the arsenals of the two greatest nuclear powers have increased on a scale which exceeds anything that could conceivably be used in battle without triggering a global holocaust. And still the arsenals are being increased, not reduced. Simultaneously with their buildup, the risk of a catastrophe due to an accidental error becomes more significant: human errors, computer errors and incorrectly interpreted signals.[2]

The principal conclusion is that the threat of nuclear war has sharply increased and that any limited use of nuclear weapons will lead to a global nuclear war.

III. Non-resort to the first use of nuclear weapons

Under these circumstances people are beginning to wonder whether it is possible, in the long run, to stop the mad arms race and to prevent the world from sliding down towards an abyss from which there is no return. They ask how to ensure that nuclear weapons are never used: what can be done to ban the use of nuclear weapons, and how confidence between states can be increased, in conditions when this confidence has already been significantly undermined.

Many governments, statesmen, public figures and politicians are genuinely concerned to prevent nuclear war, and are engaged in an active search for realistic and effective measures that could halt the slide towards danger and reverse it.

An important place within the set of such measures is assigned to the commitment not to be the first to use nuclear weapons.

The Soviet commitment to no-first-use

The Soviet Union, so far unilaterally, has assumed a commitment to no-first-use. The commitment took effect from the moment Leonid Brezhnev's message was made public from the rostrum of the Second Special Session of the UN General Assembly on Disarmament.[3] The USSR regards this commitment not as an isolated act but rather as a component of broader measures leading to the cessation of the nuclear arms race, curtailment of nuclear arsenals, prevention of nuclear war and confidence building between states. The urgency of this step in the present situation is dictated by the growing threat of nuclear war and the awareness of the need for concrete and effective measures to prevent it. The new Soviet initiative is essentially a logical continuation of Soviet foreign policy, a natural stage in the development of its military policy and its defensive military doctrine.

In November 1976 the Soviet Union together with the other WTO countries tabled a proposal to conclude a treaty on non-resort to the first use of nuclear weapons by all states participant to the Conference on Security and Co-operation in Europe. In reply to this, the West said that implementation of this proposal would increase the likelihood of war with the use of conventional armaments alone. To meet these points, the USSR in 1979 proposed an agreement on non-resort to the use of both nuclear and conventional armaments. Such an agreement would be tantamount to a non-aggression pact between all the participants of the Helsinki Conference. Both these proposals, however, failed to elicit a positive response from the West and were left in the air. A commitment not to be the first to use nuclear weapons constitutes a further substantive development of Article 1 of the UN General Assembly Declaration on the Prevention of Nuclear Catastrophe,[4] which proclaimed that states and statesmen who would be the first to use nuclear weapons would commit the gravest crime against humanity. The Soviet Union's decision not to be the first to use nuclear weapons has a universal character. The USSR had also previously expressed its readiness not to employ nuclear weapons against states which forgo production and acquisition of such weapons and do not have them on their territories. Now the Soviet commitment covers all states, without exception.

This commitment not to be the first to use nuclear weapons must be regarded as an important milestone in the struggle to prevent nuclear war, to outlaw nuclear weapons, to discontinue their production and to gradually reduce their stockpiles until their final liquidation: in other words, an important milestone on the route to nuclear disarmament. It is, however, a bold step, since it has been adopted in conditions when the NATO countries, and above all the USA, make no secret of the fact that their military doctrine not only fails to rule out eventual first use of nuclear weapons, but is actually based on this dangerous assumption. Were other states to assume a similar clear-cut commitment not to be the first to use nuclear weapons, this would amount in practice to a general ban on the use of nuclear weapons—a ban which is advocated by most countries in the world. The likelihood of a nuclear war would then be reduced to nil.

What would be the political and military implications of such a decision? How would it affect the international situation and the relations between East and West?

No-first-use and the international situation

On the political plane, such a commitment would, above all, have a favourable effect in building confidence between states and thus in improving the international situation as a whole.

Various proposals and ideas have been put forward for further confidence-building measures. Against a background of a growing nuclear threat and a deteriorating international situation, the object of these measures is to prevent the danger of unexpected war as a result of an incorrect assessment of the situation, miscalculation or technical error. Proposals to date include improvement of the direct communication line between the USSR and the USA, prior notification of tests of new or experimental missiles, a greater exchange of information, and so on. There are also far-reaching suggestions from the Soviet Union. They provide, for example, for mutual restrictions on the operation of aircraft-carriers and heavy bombers in certain agreed areas; restrictions on the scale of military exercises; and concrete confidence-building measures in designated areas of, for example, the Mediterranean Sea, the Far East, and the Persian Gulf. Complete or partial adoption of these proposals would enhance trust and improve the general climate of relations; so far, however, little progress has been made with them.

The commitment not to be the first to use nuclear weapons, however, would give the green light to these and other proposals, since both sides would be confident that neither envisages resort to the first use of nuclear weapons. The commitment would not, of course, amount to complete and unqualified trust between countries. But it would give a totally new dimension to the operation of the US–Soviet direct communication line, and the intentions of each side would be assessed differently; at present each side views the other with acute suspicion, and assesses the other's intentions only by the 'worst scenario' yardstick. Many suspicions would be dispelled, and the possibilities for miscalculation or incorrect assessment of intentions would be sharply reduced. Such a decision would create a more favourable atmosphere in the world also for examining the entire set of issues concerned with disarmament. The only task then would be how to use this atmosphere more effectively in the interests of mutual security.

The commitment not to be the first to use nuclear weapons, if assumed by all nuclear powers, would have a particularly favourable effect in improving the political situation in Europe. NATO's policy on the first use of nuclear weapons applies particularly to Europe; that is why it is over Europe that there hangs the ominous shadow of this threat. In this region, where there is an unheard-of concentration of troops and armaments, both nuclear and non-nuclear, the commitment not to be the first to use nuclear weapons would have a beneficial effect on the entire system of relationships between states; it would enhance the scope for adopting bold decisions to reduce the level of military confrontation substantially; it would bolster military and political stability at lower levels of armed forces and armaments and with a lower military spending. Conclusion of such an agreement would contribute to a reduction in the nuclear confrontation in Europe, and to a gradual lessening and eventual disappearance of the stimulus for the buildup of these armaments by states on the European continent; and it could lead eventually to the adoption of non-nuclear strategies.

The prohibition of the first use of nuclear weapons would not prevent the defending side from using its right to a retaliatory nuclear strike, if the attacking side has used its nuclear weapons. By violating the commitments assumed, the aggressor would thus not only have committed a crime against humanity, but would also relieve the defending side of complying with the limitations on the use of nuclear weapons envisaged under the treaty.

Consequently, the commitment not to be the first to use nuclear weapons would not undermine the US nuclear guarantees to the European NATO countries, since these weapons could be used in the event of a nuclear attack on the NATO countries. Such a commitment would not prejudice allied obligations of this kind. Many Western experts and politicians are known to hold this view.[5]

No-first-use and non-proliferation

A universal application of the principle of non-resort to the first use of nuclear weapons would also contribute to implementing the numerous proposals for the establishment of nuclear weapon-free zones. It would, doubtless, help strengthen the non-proliferation regime; the non-nuclear states would come to a different assessment of the way in which nuclear states had fulfilled their commitments under the non-proliferation treaty; in this way, the 'horizontal' as well as the 'vertical' proliferation of nuclear weapons would be constrained.

This is in no way an exhaustive list of some of the political gains from the renunciation of the first use of nuclear weapons.

Military-strategic implications

What is the concrete effect for the Soviet armed forces of the commitment not to be the first to use nuclear weapons? An answer to this question was given by the Soviet Defence Minister, Marshal of the Soviet Union Dmitry Ustinov. He writes: "It means that henceforward, in the training of the Armed Forces, even more attention will be given to the task of preventing a military conflict from going nuclear; these tasks, in all their variety, are becoming an integral part of our military activity".[6] In order to implement the commitment, a strict regimen has been established for the training of troops and staffs, for deciding on the weapons they should deploy, and for tightening still further the control over nuclear weapons, to ensure that there is absolutely no possibility of unauthorized launching of nuclear weapons of any kind, tactical or strategic.

Of course, if other nuclear powers assumed a similar commitment, further substantial measures could be taken in the military field, aimed at implementing this agreement. All the elements of military activity of nuclear states would eventually be affected. Naturally, it will not be simple to achieve all this: it will need serious efforts, a change in psychology, and a change in strategic thinking. The nuclear epoch has now lasted for almost 40 years; it leaves behind a trail not only of huge nuclear arsenals (with their embodied threat of universal destruction), but also of military-strategic concepts and concrete plans based on the use of nuclear weapons; it will not be easy to change these.

It would be necessary, in this connection, to revise a number of obsolete military-strategic views and concepts, primarily those of NATO, about the first use of nuclear weapons. Much has already been written in the Western press about the fact that this concept has become obsolete; that it still relies on assessments of the alignment of forces which are no longer valid. It would gradually lead to a switch from a nuclear to a non-nuclear strategy.

A commitment by nuclear states not to be the first to use nuclear weapons would lead to a curtailment of the programmes for developing and improving the nuclear arsenals; it would in the first place affect the military programmes involving the acquisition of the so-called counterforce potential—the most destabilizing systems, since they lead to fears of a first strike. Such systems would no longer have a raison d'être, and it should be easier to come to an agreement to limit them. It would also be easier to conclude an agreement to freeze both the quantitative and qualitative arms race.

If the first use of nuclear weapons were renounced, the only acceptable use of nuclear weapons would be in retaliation to nuclear aggression. The adoption of this principle should lead to quantitative reductions in nuclear weapons and limitations on their qualitative improvement. It should be possible then to avoid serious misunderstandings due to insufficient understanding or incorrect interpretation by each side of the other's strategic concepts; incorrect assessments of the other side's plans and intentions could be eliminated.

IV. The present debate

The question of non-resort to the first use of nuclear weapons is currently being extensively debated in the West; many newspapers and journals have given broad coverage to this topic.[7] Interest in the problem continues unabated, and this is clearly not fortuitous. In part, this has been due to the fact that a commitment to renounce the first use of nuclear weapons calls for a revision of the NATO military doctrine adopted in the mid-1960s, known as 'flexible response'. First use of nuclear weapons by NATO is one constituent concept of this doctrine. The revision of long-established military-strategic doctrines is a difficult and painstaking exercise, the more so because many of those responsible for their elaboration and adoption are still captives of obsolete dogmas and stereotypes, and are reluctant to adjust to new situations. So they oppose the adoption of this new proposal, saying that it would do irreparable damage to NATO security.

In April 1982 the then US Secretary of State Haig opposed the renunciation of the concept of the first use of nuclear weapons, and in May 1982 a meeting of NATO foreign ministers once again approved the concept as a component of NATO military doctrine. However, many responsible politicians, public figures and military authorities have arrived at the natural conclusion that the time has come to revise this NATO doctrine.

World political trends

The argument mirrors the struggle between two trends, two tendencies in world politics. On the one hand, there are those who recognize that there will be no winner in a nuclear war, and that the present-day conditions make it all but impossible to achieve military-strategic superiority. That is why the military-strategic concepts relying on the use of nuclear weapons are extremely dangerous, and have to be revised. So they accept the renunciation of first use.

On the other hand there are those who, while superficially conceding the catastrophic consequences of nuclear war, in actual fact continue to hope that they can achieve nuclear superiority; they do not deviate an inch from the strategic concepts which they adopted at a time when such a superiority in fact existed. At the same time they are engaged in a painstaking search for ways to make nuclear weapons, in the new conditions, more 'credible' and 'acceptable'. They are engaged in a bid to restore their former superiority. The decision to deploy Pershing II and cruise missiles in Europe is part of such an attempt.

NATO strategy

Let us, however, come back to the NATO concept of first use of nuclear weapons. What does the concept boil down to? In a speech, the US Defense Secretary said that US and NATO strategy provides for the first use of nuclear weapons if this is deemed necessary.[8]

When would it be deemed necessary? General Rogers, NATO Supreme Allied Commander in Europe, stated that in the event of a conflict they would have to resort to the use of nuclear weapons almost immediately.

Under what conditions would this occur?

Four prominent West Germans give the following answer to this question: the only likely situation for this is when a major assault by WTO conventional forces has failed to be contained by the conventional forces of the West; in this event NATO would be forced to use its nuclear weapons on a limited scale—a small number of small weapons, possibly simply as a warning (demonstration) nuclear blast. It is held that such a 'limited' use of nuclear weapons would not trigger a larger nuclear conflict. All hopes are pinned on indications that "both sides would be extremely cautious".[9]

When this concept was first adopted, the NATO leaders proceeded from two basic assumptions. The first was that WTO countries possess an edge over NATO countries in conventional forces, and therefore NATO countries would be unable to contain an aggression with their conventional forces. The second assumption was that the USA possessed a superiority in nuclear weapons and the means of their delivery. That was why the threat of the first use of nuclear weapons by NATO was supposed to serve as a deterrent against the other side. This was not, however, just a mere threat: there have existed and still exist concrete plans for the 'first' use of nuclear weapons.

So what has changed since the adoption of this concept? To begin with, sufficient time has passed for the peoples of Europe to see that the WTO countries do not have aggressive designs or plans, and that the argument implying a possibility that WTO countries would attack NATO countries is totally false. It has never been the intention of the WTO countries to threaten invasion of any state or group of states. They have repeatedly proposed that the two sides conclude a non-aggression pact, dismantle their military organizations on a reciprocal basis or disband them altogether. This proposal, however, was rejected by the NATO countries.

The balance of forces in Europe

An especially complex issue is the one of the alignment of conventional armed forces between NATO and the WTO. Its complexity is not confined solely to the factual side of the matter—the lack of mutually acceptable criteria for comparing these forces, their differing structures, the different tactical and technical characteristics of the weapons possessed by each side but also to such imponderable factors as troop morale, combat readiness, and so on. The complexity is also due to another important aspect of the problem, which could be described as traditional-psychological. In certain Western quarters a false perception has been long established and deliberately maintained about a WTO superiority in conventional weapons; this perception is frequently accepted in the West without any serious analysis or assessment. A more realistic view of things suggests that there is now a rough parity, in conventional weapons, between NATO and the WTO. This fact has been recognized by many Western politicians and military experts.

The London International Institute for Strategic Studies had this to say about the balance of conventional forces: "Assessing the balance between NATO and the Warsaw Pact based on a comparison of manpower, combat units or equipment contains a large element of subjectivity. In the first place, the Pact has superiority in some areas and NATO in other and there is no fully satisfactory way to compare these asymmetrical advantages".[10] Further, the general balance remains such that an attempt at military aggression is extremely risky and that "there would still appear to be insufficient overall strength on either side to guarantee victory".[10]

Jonathan Dean, former head of the US delegation to the Mutual and Balanced Force Reductions talks, 1978–81, who is well aware of the true state of affairs, writes: "NATO forces in central Europe have important advantages in specific areas . . . the balance is decidedly less unfavourable for the West than is often assumed".[11] The argument asserting WTO superiority in conventional forces, adduced to justify the need to preserve the concept of the first use of nuclear weapons, is groundless and specious.

Soviet Defence Minister Ustinov said this: "As regards assessing the balance of the conventional forces of the sides, it is a more complex matter, since the Warsaw Treaty has more forces and means of certain types, while NATO—of others . . . On the whole, however, there is also a clear rough parity of forces with respect to conventional armaments".[12]

Of course, the level of confrontation between the two military groupings is still very high, and the peoples of Europe wish to see their security safeguarded not through raising the level further but rather through its gradual reduction.

As regards the nuclear superiority of the United States, this superiority has been irrevocably lost and is a thing of the past. There exists a rough parity in the strategic field, and attempts to gain an edge at the strategic or regional levels are doomed to failure. Further, any limited use of nuclear weapons at a strategic or regional level will inevitably lead to a limited nuclear conflict spilling over into an all-out nuclear war.

V. Conclusion

The conclusion from this review of the arguments can only be that the NATO concept on the first use of nuclear weapons has become hopelessly obsolete, and instead of guaranteeing security creates a situation of uncertainty and lack of confidence, and increases the threat of nuclear war.

It would not be correct, however, to reduce the whole problem of renouncing the first use of nuclear weapons solely to the problem of NATO forgoing this concept. It is undoubtedly true that such a renunciation would have a salutary and stabilizing effect on the situation in Europe. This is, however, only one aspect of the whole problem. What is at issue is giving up the first use of nuclear weapons in general, both on a strategic or regional plane, whether it is after the start of hostilities with the use of conventional weapons, or for inflicting a crippling blow, or for achieving a limited objective, by way of demonstration or to hit specific targets, and so on. The need is to outlaw the first use of nuclear weapons—to exclude it from politics, from concrete military plans, from all kinds of strategic concepts and from the training of troops and staffs, to exclude it from the scenarios of war games and exercises, and to find ways to make this decision a part of military programmes. It is the need to regard nuclear weapons, while they are still a part of the nuclear arsenals of states, only as a means for a retaliatory strike, a means of response to nuclear aggression. The first use of nuclear weapons should be regarded as the gravest crime against humanity, justifying nuclear retaliation. The long-term objective of a commitment not to be the first to use nuclear weapons is, of course, to achieve an eventual renunciation of the use of nuclear weapons in general. Such an objective is a long way off; a commitment not to be the first to use nuclear weapons is the valuable first step.

Notes and references

1   *New York Times*, 15 November 1982.
2   *Los Angeles Times*, 23 November 1982.
3   UN document A/S-12/PV.12, 15 June 1982, pp. 28–30.
4   UN Resolution 36/100.
5   Bundy, McG. *et al.* 'Nuclear weapons and the Atlantic Alliance', reproduced in this book, pp. 29–41.
6   *Pravda*, 12 July 1982.
7   See, for example, *Foreign Affairs*, Vol. 60, Nos 4, 5, 6, 1982, and *Foreign Policy*, No. 48, Fall 1982.
8   *Department of Defense Annual Report FY 1980* (US Government Printing Office, Washington, D.C., 1979), p. 86.
9   Kaiser, K. *et al.*, 'Nuclear weapons and the preservation of peace', reproduced in this book, pp. 43–53.
10 *The Military Balance 1982–1983* (International Institute for Strategic Studies, London, 1982), p. 131.
11 Dean, J., 'Beyond first use', *Foreign Policy*, No. 48, Fall 1982, pp. 43, 47.
12 *Pravda*, 7 December 1982.

Paper 9.   Should the United States commit itself not to be the first to use nuclear weapons?

Paul C. Warnke

Former Director of the US Arms Control and Disarmament Agency and US Chief Negotiator for the Strategic Arms Limitation Talks, 1977–78; now at Clifford & Warnke, Attorneys and Councillors at Law, Washington, D.C., USA

I. Introduction

Views on the no-first-use issue are affected by differences both in geography and in strategic nuclear philosophy. A declaration by the United States that it would never use nuclear weapons first is bound to be of greater concern to western European allies than to citizens of the United States and Canada. It is a tribute to the durability of the NATO Alliance that it has been able to survive the inherent conflicts of interest attributable to the different geographical locations of its members.

Of even greater significance, however, is the difference in views within the United States arising from the widely divergent perspectives on the utility and versatility of nuclear weapons themselves. Those who see nuclear weapons as serving a single, limited, but vital purpose—that is, deterring the use or threatened use of an adversary's nuclear weapons—can look with equanimity at a no-first-use declaration. But those who see nuclear weapons as simply the newest and most powerful kind of military weapon, to be incorporated into a war-winning strategy and capable of extended deterrence of conventional warfare and international adventurism, regard any suggestion of eschewing their first use as the most malign of heresies.

II. US and European views on no-first-use

Because they share a continent with the Soviet Union, and because they can recall the terrible devastation caused by two conventional wars in Europe in the 20th century, Europeans think in terms of immaculate deterrence. In an exchange at a session of NATO's Nuclear Planning Group some 15 years ago, the defence ministers of the UK and FR Germany agreed that those who had seen the cities of Cologne and Coventry after conventional fire bomb attacks were perhaps less appalled than North Americans about the prospect of use of tactical nuclear weapons.

A prolonged conventional war in Europe, given the immense increase in sophistication and destructive power of conventional weaponry in the past three decades, would largely destroy that small and congested continent. Deterrence, if it is to mean salvation for its population, must include deterrence of any major war.

Moreover, development of the conventional forces that would make it apparent to a Soviet leadership inclined towards territorial conquest that it could not prevail seems to most European strategists impossible both economically and politically. Accordingly, as set forth eloquently by Kaiser *et al.*, a US no-first-use declaration is feared as making conventional war more probable. Instead, they would substitute a no-early-first-use policy and some strengthening of conventional capability in order to raise the nuclear threshold.[1]

It probably will be possible on this issue again to compromise the differences that stem from the fact that the Atlantic Ocean separates the members of the Western Alliance. Indeed, so long as both sides deploy thousands of tactical nuclear weapons in close proximity to the borders that divide the NATO countries from those of the WTO, statements by the leaders of either side that they will not be the first to utilize them are of little practical value. In the event of serious military action, with the tactical nuclear weapons of one or both sides in danger of imminent overrun, neither could have any confidence that the other's pledge of nuclear restraint would be considered binding.

It is, however, entirely possible to exchange plausible pledges of no-first-use of strategic nuclear warheads. By that I mean that the USA and the USSR could accept and believe reciprocal statements that neither would be first to launch nuclear warheads against the territory of the other side. I believe that most officials in both Moscow and Washington have in the past recognized the tacit existence of such a policy.

In a war game, a conventional Soviet assault on western Europe might be terminated by US destruction of a limited number of strategic targets in the Soviet Union. But in a real war, a US President and his advisors would have to consider that a few nuclear warheads exploded on Soviet targets would do nothing to diminish the Soviet strategic retaliatory capability and that such escalation to a strategic nuclear level could trigger a far less limited response against NATO countries, and primarily the United States. The argument would thus be made in a crisis that nuclear punishment for Soviet conventional aggression must be designed to destroy the maximum possible number of Soviet missile launchers and to incapacitate Soviet command, control and communications. Compared to the hope of ending a conventional war by defence or diplomacy, the incalculable consequences of first strategic use make it, at the very least, a highly unlikely option.

To say this is undoubtedly to fuel the fears of the USA's Western allies that the nuclear umbrella provides something less than total protection. Even when that nuclear umbrella was new, General Charles de Gaulle was not alone in questioning whether the United States would sacrifice Chicago in order to save Berlin, or even Paris.

But this is not to say that the nuclear umbrella is a far-fetched fiction or that it would dissolve in heavy weather. A US strategic nuclear response to nuclear missile attacks on any of the NATO allies would, of course, not be precluded in any declaration that the United States will not use strategic nuclear weapons first. Under the NATO Charter, an attack on one is an attack on all and any 'no-first-strategic-use' announcement should be accompanied by the reassertion of assured strategic nuclear retaliation for any nuclear strike against any member of the NATO Alliance.

III. First use of tactical nuclear weapons

Not all of these considerations, however, are applicable to the question of declaring that the United States would not be the first to use tactical nuclear weapons. I include in that definition those weapons, and only those weapons, that would be used against Soviet forces involved in invading NATO territory. The simplest and perhaps only definition of a tactical nuclear weapon is that it is one that will probably blow up in a friendly country. For this kind of weapon, the Soviets have a complete defence: they need not invade in the first place and, if they have made that mistake, they can still reconsider and go back home.

The use of US battlefield nuclear weapons in FR Germany or elsewhere in western Europe would do no damage to the citizenry, the industry, or the strategic retaliatory capability of the Soviet Union. Unlike a strategic attack, it would not be a grim harbinger of more to follow. Nor would it indicate to your opponent that you have gone mad and must be destroyed before your irrationality leads to greater horrors. The collateral damage of a US tactical nuclear weapon would be inflicted on the inhabitants and facilities of a US ally, or the blameless citizens of an eastern European satellite.

This, of course, is not to play down the gravity and escalatory potential of any use even of tactical battlefield nuclear weapons. When consideration has to be given to such use, because of the magnitude of a conventional assault, one weapon in all likelihood will not be thought to be enough. The theory of a demonstration strike—ostensibly to show determination and the lack of nuclear inhibition—has little appeal to a military commander. And if the nuclear threshold is to be crossed, both civilian and military officials are unlikely to counsel doing so in a fashion that would inflict only token damage on the invading forces.

Accordingly, a decision for first use of battlefield nuclear weapons almost surely would involve explosion of a number of nuclear warheads in the territory of NATO Europe. Some of these warheads approach the size of the atom bombs that levelled Hiroshima and Nagasaki. The prognosis for the effects of protracted tactical nuclear warfare in western Europe is thus about as dire as that of a strategic nuclear missile exchange.

Without doubt, any first use of battlefield nuclear weapons carries an inescapable risk of employment of Soviet battlefield nuclear shells and missiles. It would, of course, be hoped that the Soviet leadership might decide to call off the conventional attack as soon as tactical nuclear weaponry came into play. Such convincing evidence that NATO is prepared to defend itself, and at such grievous cost, could lead to reconsideration and withdrawal. But the appalling breakdown in East–West relations that would have to precede any Soviet invasion, and the strong likelihood that an invasion decision would only be reached if the Soviet leadership believed their country's vital interests to be at stake, make such reconsideration far from certain.

Moreover, even the responsive use of Soviet nuclear weapons on a western European battlefield would mark the end of any real chance that nuclear war would remain limited. If, as I have defined the logical categories, nuclear weapons can be considered tactical only when used outside the enemy's homeland, then a Soviet battlefield nuclear response would obliterate the distinction. Whether the Soviet nuclear warhead that destroys a NATO target were launched from the Soviet Union, from eastern Europe, or from Soviet forces operating in NATO territory, it would fit the strategic definition and thus call for a strategic nuclear response against targets in the USSR.

The no-first-use issue is thus one that merits and unquestionably will receive extensive debate within the NATO Alliance. This debate, however, will not necessarily expose irreconcilable doctrinal differences. The idea of a resolution acceptable to the participants does not stagger the imagination.

IV. Nuclear strategies

More basic and more bitter is the argument about the purposes that nuclear weapons can be expected to serve. For those who consider mutual assured destruction as an inescapable fact and not just a theory, an announced decision that they will be used only in retaliation seems quite logical. But for those who believe that nuclear weapons can be used flexibly to advance national purposes, a no-first-use policy can never be acceptable.

This argument is as old as nuclear weapons themselves and it has never really been settled. In the opinion of those who espouse a nuclear war-fighting capability, the search for strategic superiority must continue and every new technological promise must be exploited.

For some, nuclear weaponry is the cornerstone of our security. Eugene Rostow, when he was Director of the US Arms Control and Disarmament Agency, called our nuclear arsenal "the rock on which the renaissance of the West since 1945 was built and the foundation for its security".[2] Under this view, the complete eradication of all nuclear weapons would be unacceptable, even if achievable. Though some adherents might phrase it in more abstruse and sophisticated terms, they are in basic agreement with Mrs Phyllis Schlafly, a key opponent of the Equal Rights Amendment, who asserts that "the atomic bomb is a marvelous gift that was given to our country by a wise God".[3]

Although proponents of a nuclear war-fighting strategy have achieved greater prominence in the Reagan years, previous administrations, both Republican and Democrat, have included officials of that persuasion. Sometimes the ability to fight a limited and protracted nuclear war is rationalized as an improvement on the deterrent against nuclear attack at any level. This was the position taken by the then Secretary of Defense James Schlesinger in 1974. It was President Carter's Secretary of Defense Harold Brown's explanation for Presidential Directive 59, although other Carter officials characterized it as a dramatic shift to a strategy whereby nuclear weaponry could be used selectively to destroy the political and military facilities most prized by the Soviet leadership.

But the real impetus for new, more accurate counterforce nuclear weapons comes largely from those who believe that superior US technology and resources can put the USA in a position to fight and win a nuclear war and, of course, the chances of winning are seen to be better if the option of striking first is preserved. Accordingly, for a nuclear utilization theorist, arms control has value only insofar as it advances the cause of strategic superiority.

However, the search for strategic advantage is incompatible with arms control. Nuclear superiority will not be won or lost at the bargaining table. An agreement unfair to one side is not apt to be achieved and, even if one party should allow itself to be out-traded, the agreement would not survive. Any new arms control agreement will contain a clause similar to that in past treaties, permitting a party to withdraw if it concludes that continuation would jeopardize its supreme interests.

History also indicates that an uncontrolled nuclear arms race would not give either superpower the ability to fight, survive and win a nuclear war. As every new development has been introduced—like the hydrogen bomb or the MIRVing of ballistic missiles—it has promptly been matched, and usually to the detriment of the security of both sides.

US Secretary of Defense Caspar Weinberger, although he repeatedly states his recognition that there can be "no winners" in a nuclear war, currently contends that the Soviets "are designing their weapons in such a way and in sufficient numbers to indicate to us that they think they could begin, and win, a nuclear war".[4] At the same time, however, official US statements and nuclear weapon programmes may lead Soviet leaders to think that the United States is planning for the forces that would implement a nuclear war-winning strategy.

In his Annual Report to Congress for Fiscal Year 1983, Secretary Weinberger explains that decisions on replacement and expansion of our strategic forces "permitted us to shape our strategic nuclear forces as a coherent instrument responsive to national policy and to eliminate some dangerous contradictions between the capabilities of our nuclear forces and the objectives of our policy". His report continues:

We recognized that, for the foreseeable future, our nuclear forces had to serve at least the following four purposes: (1) to deter nuclear attack on the United States or its allies;

125

(2) to help deter major conventional attack against U.S. forces and our allies, especially in NATO; (3) *to impose termination of a major war—on terms favorable to the United States and our allies—even if nuclear weapons have been used*—and in particular to deter escalation in the level of hostilities; and (4) to negate possible Soviet nuclear blackmail against the United States and our allies.[5]

Somewhat more expansively, the US Defense Department Guidance 1984–88, leaked to the *New York Times* in spring 1982, set forth the strategy that "should deterrence fail and strategic nuclear war with the USSR occur, the United States must prevail and be able to force the Soviet Union to seek earliest termination of hostilities on terms favorable to the United States".[6]

If these official Defense Department documents accurately describe current US nuclear strategy, then obviously a no-first-use declaration cannot be contemplated. US forces would, instead, be shaped to fight and win a nuclear war—an objective that Secretary Weinberger charges the Soviets with seeking; an objective that both President Reagan and he have told the world they know to be unobtainable.

The thrust of these policy statements is to move away from traditional deterrence theory and towards a strategy of 'extended deterrence'. The role of nuclear arms would be expanded to one of general peace-keeping. It might be noted that President Reagan has sought to rechristen the MX as the 'Peacekeeper' missile. Largely obscured by the debate about its mode of deployment is the nature of the missile itself. Its 10 highly accurate warheads can, in theory, destroy hard Soviet targets such as ICBM silos.

As set forth in Secretary Weinberger's Annual Report, the minimum purposes of US nuclear weapons would include that of responding to Soviet use of conventional military power. And, since it is strategic nuclear forces that are being discussed in this portion of the Report, the implication is that a nuclear first strike against the Soviet Union would not be foreclosed. Indeed, if nuclear weaponry is to be designed to fight and win a nuclear war, it would be illogical to forfeit the option of striking first and thus eroding the Soviet nuclear arsenal.

This view of nuclear weaponry as a 'coherent' and 'responsive' instrument would seem also to preclude any meaningful negotiated restrictions. If nuclear arms are fundamental to US and Western security, then they could not be given up even if the total, verifiable elimination of such weapons were within reach.

Arms control aims at equal security through nuclear parity. It is thus incompatible with a nuclear war-fighting strategy. In all likelihood, many if not most opponents of a no-first-use commitment do not knowingly support the quest for nuclear superiority but are worried instead that such a declaratory policy would erode deterrence. Even those who see victory in a nuclear war as the legitimate and achievable aim of nuclear force design and strategic doctrine pay lip service to the deterrence rationale. But all the two schools of thought have in common is the rejection of a commitment against first use.

The Reagan Administration's new stress on acquiring a nuclear war-fighting capability has had one prompt and practical result: it has polarized the debate about strategic nuclear policy. In western Europe, it has inspired a movement that may well go beyond advocacy of no-first-use to the espousal of a nuclear weapon-free Europe and rejection of US nuclear protection.

V. Conclusion

Those who believe that a commitment not to use nuclear weapons first would improve Western security for the most part acknowledge that adoption of such a policy should await full debate among the NATO allies and the development of a consensus. But those who believe that US interests may require the initiation of nuclear war against the Soviet Union seem markedly less sensitive to the feelings of US allies. Their search for the kind of nuclear supremacy that could make first use a plausible threat may deprive the United States of its major security advantage over the Soviet Union—an alliance of like-minded nations based on mutual confidence and respect.

References

[1] Kaiser, K. *et al.*, 'Nuclear weapons and the preservation of peace', reproduced in this book, pages 43–53.
[2] Rostow, E., address before the Los Angeles World Affairs Council, *Current Policy*, No. 425, US Department of State, Bureau of Public Affairs, 19 September 1982.
[3] Phyllis Schlafly, quoted in an article by Lyn Rosellini, *New York Times*, 30 June 1982.
[4] Weinberger, C., letter to the *Los Angeles Times*, 25 August 1982.
[5] Weinberger, C., *FY 1983 Report of the Secretary of Defense to the Congress* (US Government Printing Office, Washington, D.C., 8 February 1982), Part I, p. 1–18 (emphasis added).
[6] *Defense Department Guidance 1984–88.*

Appendix I. Declarations on security assurances to non-nuclear weapon states made by the five nuclear weapon states

China

Pending the realization of complete prohibition and thorough destruction of nuclear weapons, all nuclear countries must undertake unconditionally not to use or threaten to use such weapons against non-nuclear countries and nuclear-free zones.

As is known to all, the Chinese Government has long declared on its own initiative and unilaterally that at no time and under no circumstances will China be the first to use nuclear weapons, and that it undertakes unconditionally not to use or threaten to use nuclear weapons against non-nuclear countries and nuclear-free zones.[1]

France

France declares that:

for its part . . . it will not use nuclear arms against a State that does not have these weapons and has pledged not to seek them, except in the case of an act of aggression carried out in association or alliance with a nuclear-weapon State against France or against a State with which France has a security commitment.[2]

It remains also ready:

to negotiate with nuclear-free zones participants in order to contract effective and binding commitments, as appropriate, precluding any use or threat of use of nuclear weapons against the States of these zones.[3]

USSR

From the rostrum of the special session our country declares that the Soviet Union will never use nuclear weapons against those States which renounce the production and acquisition of such weapons and do not have them on their territories.

We are aware of the responsibility which would thus fall on us as a result of such a commitment. But we are convinced that such a step to meet the wishes of non-nuclear States to have stronger security guarantees is in the interests of peace in the broadest sense of the word. We expect that the goodwill evinced by our country in this manner will

129

lead to more active participation by a large number of States in strengthening the non-proliferation régime.

The Soviet Union is prepared to enter into an appropriate bilateral agreement with any non-nuclear State. We call upon all the other nuclear Powers to follow our example.[4]

United Kingdom

The United Kingdom is now ready formally to give . . . the following assurance . . . to non-nuclear-weapon States which are parties to the Non-Proliferation Treaty or to other internationally binding commitments not to manufacture or acquire nuclear explosive devices: Britain undertakes not to use nuclear weapons against such States except in the case of an attack on the United Kingdom, its dependent territories, its armed forces, or its allies by such a State in association or alliance with a nuclear-weapon State.[5]

United States

The United States will not use nuclear weapons against any non-nuclear-weapon State party to the Non-Proliferation Treaty or any comparable internationally binding commitment not to acquire nuclear explosive devices, except in the case of an attack on the United States, its territories or armed forces, or its allies, by such a State allied to or associated with a nuclear-weapon State in carrying out or sustaining the attack.[6]

References

1 UN document A/S-12/11, 4 May 1982.
2 UN document A/S-12/PV.9, 11 June 1982, p. 69.
3 Committee on Disarmament document CD/SA/WP.2, 25 June 1980.
4 Official Records of the UN General Assembly Tenth Special Session, Plenary Meetings, Verbatim Records, 5th meeting, 26 May 1978, p. 78, paras 84–86.
5 Committee on Disarmament document CD/177, 10 April 1981.
6 Committee on Disarmament document CD/PV.152, 9 February 1982, p. 15.

Appendix II. Additional Protocol II to the Treaty for the Prohibition of Nuclear Weapons in Latin America (Treaty of Tlatelolco)

The undersigned Plenipotentiaries, furnished with full powers by their respective Governments,

Convinced that the Treaty for the Prohibition of Nuclear Weapons in Latin America, negotiated and signed in accordance with the recommendations of the General Assembly of the United Nations in Resolution 1911 (XVIII) of 27 November 1963, represents an important step towards ensuring the non-proliferation of nuclear weapons,

Aware that the non-proliferation of nuclear weapons is not an end in itself but, rather, a means of achieving general and complete disarmament at a later stage, and

Desiring to contribute, so far as lies in their power, towards ending the armaments race, especially in the field of nuclear weapons, and towards promoting and strengthening a world at peace, based on mutual respect and sovereign equality of States,

Have agreed as follows:

Article I

The statute of denuclearization of Latin America in respect of warlike purposes, as defined, delimited and set forth in the Treaty for the Prohibition of Nuclear Weapons in Latin America of which this instrument is an annex, shall be fully respected by the parties to this Protocol in all its express aims and provisions.

Article 2

The Governments represented by the undersigned Plenipotentiaries undertake, therefore, not to contribute in any way to the performance of acts involving a violation of the obligations of article 1 of the Treaty in the territories to which the Treaty applies in accordance with article 4 thereof.

Article 3

The Governments represented by the undersigned Plenipotentiaries also undertake not to use or threaten to use nuclear weapons against the Contracting Parties of the Treaty for the Prohibition of Nuclear Weapons in Latin America.

Article 4

The duration of this Protocol shall be the same as that of the Treaty for the Prohibition of Nuclear Weapons in Latin America of which this Protocol is an annex, and the definitions of territory and nuclear weapons set forth in articles 3 and 5 of the Treaty shall be applicable to this Protocol, as well as the provisions regarding ratification, reservations, denunciation, authentic texts and registration contained in articles 26, 27, 30 and 31 of the Treaty.

Article 5

This Protocol shall enter into force, for the States which have ratified it, on the date of the deposit of their respective instruments of ratification.

Source: Goldblat, J., *Agreements for Arms Control, A Critical Survey*, SIPRI (Taylor & Francis, London, 1982), pp. 169–70.

Appendix III.   References to the no-first-use of nuclear weapons made in the general debate of UNSSOD II
(listed alphabetically by country)

Afghanistan

Where, then, is the way out of the present impasse?

In our firm opinion it is to be found along the road of the implementation of previously approved recommendations and decisions of the United Nations General Assembly, including those of its first special session on disarmament. An important step aimed at averting the danger of nuclear war was the adoption by the thirty-sixth session of the United Nations General Assembly of the Declaration on the Prevention of Nuclear Catastrophe, which declares the first use of nuclear weapons to be the gravest crime against humanity. If all the nuclear States followed this Declaration and refused to use nuclear weapons first, there would be no first, nor second, nor third nuclear strikes and thus there would be no nuclear war.[1]

Angola

That opinion is based on the firm conviction of the Government of the People's Republic of Angola that no socialist or progressive country, no country that cherishes peace and justice, would start a nuclear war or use other weapons of mass destruction, because the survival of mankind, international peace and security and the independence of peoples are for such countries principles and objectives of prime importance.[2]

Barbados

Many and varied are the formulas proposed for achieving the desired goal of international disarmament as an indispensable factor for world peace. To some, the way to go is by declaring non-first-use. To others, verification and inspection are crucial.[3]

Benin

The most modest step towards disarmament and peace is much more important for us than the sonority or literary elegance of any propaganda or pronouncements of might and power. It is for that reason that Benin welcomes the historic and positive commitment made here by the Soviet Union not to be the first to use nuclear weapons. We are also pleased at the Chinese decision to undertake to reduce its nuclear arms programme if the two super-Powers set the example by reducing their own arsenals by 50 per cent.[4]

Bulgaria

We warmly welcome the obligation assumed by the USSR not to be the first to use nuclear weapons, a decision announced in the message of Leonid Ilych Brezhnev to this special session of the General Assembly. This is a further clear manifestation of the peace-loving nature of Soviet foreign policy. We hope that this extremely important step, aimed at averting nuclear war, will be followed by reciprocal steps by the other nuclear States.[5]

Byelorussia

Leonid Brezhnev's message reflects not only the aspirations of the Soviet people but also those of people in all corners of the world and manifests the concern to halt the endless build-up of ever more destructive types of weapons, achieve a breakthrough in improving international relations, raise the degree of trust among nations and prevent nuclear catastrophe. The solemn statement that the Soviet Union pledges not to be the first to use nuclear weapons would lead to the total elimination of those weapons—which the majority of the countries of the world desire—if a similar commitment were made by the other nuclear Powers.[6]

Canada

Periodically some people call for a commitment from us not to be the first to use nuclear weapons. I understand rather well those who make such a request, because they are concerned about the horrible consequences of nuclear warfare.

I would simply point out here that the Charter already prohibits the first use of force—the use of any force. That is the law that binds us. I therefore see no usefulness in repromulgating the Charter. I do believe, however, that it would be very dangerous to weaken one of its fundamental principles by creating the impression that there is an order of priority among the various uses of force.[7]

China

An agreement should be reached by all the nuclear States not to use nuclear weapons. Pending such an agreement, each nuclear State should, without attaching any condition, undertake not to use nuclear weapons against non-nuclear States and nuclear-weapon-free zones, and not to be the first to use such weapons against each other at any time and under any circumstances. . . .

In point of fact, the Chinese Government has long since repeatedly pledged to the world that at no time and under no circumstances will China be the first to use nuclear weapons and that it undertakes unconditionally not to use such weapons against non-nuclear States.[8]

Cuba

We hail here the message of Leonid I. Brezhnev communicated here yesterday that the USSR commits itself, in a unilateral and immediate way, not to be the first to use nuclear weapons. . . .

In the face of the persistence in accusing the Soviet Union of being guilty of fostering nuclear imbalance, George Kennan, a prominent United States politician who for decades has been in the very centre of relations between the United States and the Soviet Union, recalled with all the weight of his authority that

'It has been we Americans who at almost every step of the road have taken the lead in the development of this sort of weaponry. It was we who first produced and tested such a device; we who were the first to raise its destructiveness to a new level with the hydrogen bomb; we who introduced multiple warheads; we who have declined every proposal for the renunciation of the principle of first use; and we alone, God help us, who have used the weapons in anger against others, and against tens of thousands of helpless non-combatants at that'.[9]

Czechoslovakia

We seek the answer to the most crucial question of the present time, namely, will mankind . . . allow itself to be dragged through unending confrontations to the very brink of a thermonuclear abyss?

We heard the answer to that question yesterday in this hall, and together with us, millions of people throughout the world heard it as well. It was contained in the message of the highest Soviet leader, Leonid Brezhnev, to our session, which included the solemn declaration that the Soviet Union assumes, with immediate effect, an obligation not to be the first to use nuclear weapons. We attach high value to this newest Soviet initiative as a concrete step along the road to averting a nuclear catastrophe. We are convinced that, if all the other nuclear Powers follow that example, the possibility of the outbreak of a nuclear war will be practically eliminated.[10]

Ecuador

The statement made by China in this Assembly, advocating a declaration not to be the first to use nuclear weapons and to guarantee the non-use of nuclear weapons against non-nuclear States was a positive step, as was the statement of the Soviet Union unilaterally committing itself not to be the first to use nuclear weapons. If such a commitment becomes unanimous among the nuclear Powers, this session of the General Assembly will not have met in vain.[11]

Ethiopia

This and the other substantive Soviet initiatives, including the unilateral undertaking not to be the first to use nuclear weapons, are not only in line with the Socialist States' commitment to peace and security through disarmament but also represent the first positive response to the public outcry for peace and disarmament throughout the world.[12]

Finland

Recently the possibility of first use of nuclear weapons in specific situations has given rise to debate. Military doctrines are adjusted to suit new arms technology. Doctrines of counter-force, limited nuclear exchange, extended deterrence, and so on, are examples of this. Such doctrines, whatever their name, stand in contrast with the widely shared view that nuclear war cannot in fact be limited. It is obvious that stability can be achieved only by taking into account all aspects of security.[13]

France

Confronted with such real dangers, Utopian or misleading solutions have too often been proposed: total nuclear disarmament; or a universal commitment to non-first-use.

Such formulas would greatly compound the threat of war as long as the imbalance in conventional arms and political dissymmetry persists in Europe. Moreover those who propose them seem to forget the essential provision of our Charter concerning the non-use of force. So what credibility could be given to proposals that would reduce the application of this basic clause to the nuclear threat alone?[14]

German Democratic Republic

Nuclear weapons pose the gravest threat to mankind. By now there are so many of them that either side could, according to calculations made by the Stockholm International Peace Research Institute (SIPRI), destroy the other a thousand times over. I say that even one single time is too many times. Therefore, the German Democratic Republic advocates that in its decisions this session should give prominence to the commitment not to be the first to use nuclear weapons. What is it actually that prevents some nuclear-weapon States from making the solemn pledge—as called for in the relevant declaration initiated by the USSR and adopted at the thirty-sixth session of the United Nations General Assembly—that they will not be the first to use nuclear weapons? After all, there are in this connexion neither legal nor verification problems.

The argument that a prohibition of the first use of nuclear weapons was favouring the use of conventional arms is not tenable either. Those who fear that need only accept the proposal put forward by the socialist States to renounce the first use of both nuclear and conventional weapons.[15]

Germany, Federal Republic of

The ban on the use of force outlaws any war; it is applicable to the use of all weapons. Not only nuclear weapons, but also conventional weapons, today have an unimaginable destructive capacity.

Those who would limit the comprehensive ban on the use of force to the first use of certain weapons appear to be saying that there may be other types of war which might be permissible. We should not accept that. There is no such thing as a just war. It is only and exclusively permissible to defend oneself against aggression from outside.[16]

Grenada

We also take note of the Soviet Union's pledge a few days ago in this very forum to renounce the first use of nuclear weapons. We see that as a constructive step.[17]

Guyana

Guyana has consistently taken the position that as a step towards the complete elimination of nuclear weapons there must be agreement among all the nuclear-weapon Powers on complete prohibition of the use or threat of use of nuclear weapons under any circumstances whatsoever. In this regard, my delegation considers that important first steps have been taken by China, followed by the Soviet Union, in their declarations on non-first-use of nuclear weapons. We hope that these will be followed by similar declarations by other nuclear-weapon States.[18]

Hungary

At its last session the General Assembly, on the initiative of the Soviet Union, adopted a declaration of outstanding importance—the Declaration on the Prevention of Nuclear Catastrophe. That significant document declared the first use of nuclear weapons to be the gravest crime against humanity . . .

We are convinced that the destruction without delay of all nuclear weapons would be the most effective way of removing the danger of nuclear war. Until that goal is achieved, we lend our full support to any intermediate, partial measures, such as outlawing the first use of nuclear weapons.[19]

Ireland

I would offer a list of points on which I believe the nuclear Powers should now be ready to act: First, they need to recognize and accept that, as one important recent article put it:

'The one clearly definable fire-break against the world-wide disaster of general nuclear war is the one that stands between all other kinds of conflict and any use whatsoever of nuclear weapons. To keep that fire-break wide and strong is in the deepest interests of all mankind.'

I believe that the nuclear Powers need to consider seriously what methods or agreements they might work out providing against the first use by any of them of nuclear weapons.[20]

Israel

The second step should be made by the nuclear Powers. They should negotiate a nuclear non-aggression pact—again, except in self-defence. They should undertake not to attack each other, or any other country, with those deadly weapons, the only exception being if they or their allies are attacked with such weapons.[21]

Jamaica

We subscribe to the proposition, already endorsed by the General Assembly, that the use of nuclear weapons under any circumstances would constitute a violation of the United Nations Charter and a crime against humanity.

In this regard, Jamaica welcomes the recent declaration by the USSR that it would never be the first to use nuclear weapons. It follows the declaration made some time ago by the People's Republic of China and therefore facilitates a general agreement. Accordingly, we call on other nuclear Powers to undertake similar commitments. In the meantime, a moratorium should be declared on any further nuclear tests.[22]

Kenya

The present special session should succeed in establishing a firm political will in all nations, and in extracting an undertaking from all nations, especially the nuclear Powers and their military alliances, to relax tensions in international relations . . . never to use nuclear weapons or start a nuclear war. . . .[23]

Lao People's Democratic Republic

In this regard, my delegation warmly welcomes the solemn unilateral commitment of the Soviet Union, in a message from President Brezhnev to this Assembly, not to be the first to use nuclear weapons. The United States Government has maintained total silence on that subject. This Soviet commitment is a further living expression of the Leninist policy of peace pursued in its entirety by the Soviet Union, which is the first socialist country in the world and was born at the very time when Lenin himself proclaimed the 'Decree on Peace'.[24]

Madagascar

At this session the General Assembly should focus its attention on the growing risks of a nuclear war and try to adopt measures to avoid such a war. To that end we could, first, give thought to the total prohibition by means of a convention of the use or threat of use of nuclear weapons and also the unilateral or joint commitment by nuclear States not to be the first to use these weapons. At the very least these States should be bound to respect and abide by commitments they have entered into under the Treaty on the Non-Proliferation of Nuclear Weapons.[25]

Mexico

The existence of military forces and nuclear weapons is justified for reasons of national security. The very use of nuclear weapons by a country would involve incalculable risks for the lives of their own nationals since it would provoke a similar response by the supposed enemy. Hence the use of nuclear weapons is rightly considered to be contrary to the defence of the national security of a country. China some time ago committed itself to not being the first to use nuclear weapons. The other nuclear Powers should adopt a similar policy and make separate declarations to this effect.[26]

Mongolia

The most important contribution of the General Assembly should be to adopt measures for removing the danger of nuclear war. In the view of the Mongolian delegation, the primary duty of the present session is to reaffirm the General Assembly Declaration on the Prevention of Nuclear Catastrophe, in which the first use of the nuclear weapon is condemned as the gravest crime against humanity. We consider that, in the spirit of this Declaration, the Governments of all nuclear-weapon States should officially declare their renunciation of the first use of nuclear weapons, as was done by the Soviet Government in the Message of Comrade Brezhnev to the second special session of the General Assembly of the United Nations on disarmament.

This unilateral obligation which became effective on 15 June this year—the day it was made public from the rostrum of the General Assembly—is a vivid manifestation of the consistent efforts of the Soviet Union to help prevent the threat of a nuclear war and to put nuclear disarmament negotiations on a practical basis. This example of historic magnitude, if followed by other nuclear-weapon Powers, would in fact mean the total prohibition of the use of nuclear weapons and thus create favourable conditions for furthering the cause of disarmament.[27]

Nepal

The doctrine of pre-emptive first strike limited to land-based missiles is only a myth; any outbreak of nuclear war on whatever scale will expose to extreme risk the very survival of the human race. However, each side claims that the other is trying for a first-strike capability, while declaring its own objective to be solely defensive. The myth is being increasingly used as a rationale for the tremendous increases in strategic weapons production and procurement, a development which defies all logic and reason.[28]

Netherlands

The European situation illustrates how difficult it is to reduce dependence on nuclear weapons once they are part of an existing regional balance. In this connexion I should like to say a few words in pursuance of the recently resumed discussions on the question of the non-first-use of nuclear weapons...

A serious non-first-use declaration can be an important confidence-building measure at a certain stage of the disarmament process, but in view of the present situation, in particular in Europe, it cannot be the first step. First we have to make progress in controlling and limiting the nuclear weapons themselves and create a stable balance between East and West in the conventional field also. This would in itself reduce the role of nuclear weapons in the over-all military posture.[29]

Nicaragua

In this context we most warmly welcome the commitment made by President Leonid Brezhnev on behalf of the people and Government of the Soviet Union that the Soviet Union will not be the first to use nuclear weapons. We see that statement as one of the most significant recent contributions to the cause of peace throughout the world.[30]

Pakistan

Pakistan fully subscribes to the proposition, already endorsed by the General Assembly, that the use of nuclear weapons under any circumstances would constitute a violation of the United Nations Charter and a crime against humanity. It remains our hope that sooner rather than later the primordial instinct for self-preservation and the imperative of preserving mankind and our civilization from annihilation will override dependence on nuclear deterrence and lead to an agreement to outlaw the use of nuclear weapons. More than a decade ago the People's Republic of China declared that it would never be the first to use nuclear weapons. Last year the Soviet Union proposed the adoption by this Assembly of a declaration against their first use. It is our understanding therefore that the Soviet Union itself is committed not to be the first to use nuclear weapons. We welcome this Soviet position, which taken together with the declaration made by China could possibly facilitate a general agreement among the nuclear Powers on this subject.[31]

Philippines

In response to the world public clamour, my delegation submits that we should, on our part, most seriously address ourselves at this session to concepts that could begin the process of preventing nuclear war such as the following: the prohibition of the use or threat of nuclear weapons, the principle of the non-first use of nuclear weapons, and credible security guarantees against the use of nuclear weapons against non-nuclear-weapon States. These are priority measures, but, ...

China has taken the lead by its declaration that it has adopted the principle of the non-first use of nuclear weapons and that it would not be the first to use nuclear weapons at any time or under any circumstances. We welcome that assurance.[32]

Romania

Romania believes that the following measures should be urgently negotiated and agreed upon:

... It is extremely important that all nuclear-weapon States should accept the firm commitment not to be the first to use such weapons.[33]

Sri Lanka

We therefore urge that this second special session on disarmament declare that neither the doctrine of, nor the continued reliance on, the nuclear deterrent is consistent with a commitment to disarmament. In today's context a call for the prohibition of the use of nuclear weapons will be strongly resisted. We should then, at least demand a joint or individual declaration by the nuclear-weapon States that they will not be the first to use nuclear weapons.[34]

Suriname

Since nuclear weapons have been unanimously recognized as posing the most serious threat to our survival, my delegation is of the view that one of the prime objectives of this session should be to agree on concrete measures to prevent the danger of the outbreak of a nuclear exchange, for it cannot be denied that this horrendous possibility is no longer as unlikely as it was believed to be a few years ago.

The first step in that direction should be for all nuclear-weapon States to renounce the first use of nuclear weapons. Such a step would undoubtedly clear the atmosphere of the deep mistrust among those countries with regard to each other's intentions and, therefore, contribute significantly to establishing a favourable climate for the conduct of disarmament negotiations.[35]

Sweden

Undertakings on the non-first-use of nuclear weapons have been discussed in this context as a conceivable way of affecting the disarmament efforts positively. Neither of the two Power blocs has forsworn the possibility of the first use of nuclear weapons. In order to make such an arrangement in Europe possible, agreements on the conventional side must obviously also be reached.[36]

Syria

The delegation of the Syrian Arab Republic wishes to express its great appreciation of and satisfaction with the Soviet declaration that the Soviet Union will not be the first to use nuclear weapons against any other country.[37]

Tunisia

In this connexion we recently heard here an encouraging statement by one of the super-Powers: a formal commitment not to be the first to use nuclear weapons. Our hope is that that statement will be followed by concrete actions to reassure the nuclear partners and to convince them to come to a comprehensive agreement banning for ever the use of nuclear weapons.[38]

Ukraine

The declaration that the Soviet Union will not be the first to use nuclear weapons, made by Leonid Brezhnev in his message to the second special session, pursues exactly this objective. That unilateral obligation assumed by the Soviet Union became effective at the moment it was made public at this session and constitutes a concrete and tangible step of exceptional importance towards averting a nuclear catastrophe.

Indeed, if all the nuclear States assumed a similar obligation—and that would be a multilateral action—then there will, in fact, be no first, second or third nuclear strike. The use of all-destructive nuclear weapons—something that is opposed by the over-whelming majority of the countries of the world—will be banned. Hence, military con-frontation will become less acute and strategic stability consolidated.[39]

Union of Soviet Socialist Republics

To the second session of the United Nations General Assembly: on behalf of the Soviet Union, on behalf of the 269 million Soviet people, I am addressing the General Assembly of the United Nations which has convened for its second special session devoted to dis-armament . . .

Guided by the desire to do all in its power to deliver the peoples from the threat of nuclear devastation and ultimately to exclude its very possibility from the life of mankind, the Soviet State solemnly declares: the Union of Soviet Socialist Republics assumes an obligation not to be the first to use nuclear weapons. This obligation shall become effective immediately, at the moment it is made public from the rostrum of the United Nations General Assembly.

Why is it that the Soviet Union is taking this step at a time when the nuclear Powers participating in the North Atlantic Treaty Organization (NATO) grouping, including the United States, make no secret of the fact that not only does their military doctrine not rule out the possibility of the first use of nuclear weapons; it is actually based on this dangerous premise?

In taking this decision, the Soviet Union proceeds from the indisputable fact, which plays a determining role in the present day international situation, that, should a nuclear war start, it could mean the destruction of human civilization and perhaps the end of life itself on earth. Consequently, the supreme duty of leaders of States, conscious of their responsibility for the destinies of the world, is to exert every effort to ensure that nuclear weapons never be used.

The peoples of the world have the right to expect that the decision of the Soviet Union will be followed by reciprocal steps on the part of the other nuclear States. If the other nuclear Powers assume an equally precise and clear obligation not to be the first to use nuclear weapons, that would be tantamount in practice to a ban on the use of nuclear weapons altogether, which is espoused by the overwhelming majority of the countries of the world.[40]

United Kingdom

Nuclear war is indeed a terrible threat; but conventional war is a terrible reality . . .

But in a crucial sense we have not reached the root of the matter. For the fundamental risk to peace is not the existence of weapons of particular types. It is the disposition on the part of some States to impose change on others by resorting to force. This is where we require action and protection. And our key need is not for promises against first use of this or that kind of military weapon; such promises can never be dependable amid the stresses of war. We need a credible assurance, if such can ever be obtained, against starting military action at all. The leaders of the North Atlantic Alliance have just given a solemn collective undertaking to precisely that effect. They said: 'None of our weapons will ever be used except in response to attack.'[41]

Viet Nam

The well-known Peace Programme, adopted by the twenty-sixth Congress of the Communist Party of the Soviet Union, and its recent proposals on disarmament, in particular the solemn commitment with immediate effect made by the Soviet Union not to be the first to use nuclear weapons that was put forward by President Leonid Brezhnev in his message to this session of the General Assembly, are new and eloquent proof that the Soviet Union has no greater interest than to spare mankind a nuclear catastrophe.[42]

References

[1] UN document A/S-12/PV.7, 12 June 1982, pp. 9–10.
[2] UN document A/S-12/PV.7, 12 June 1982, p. 51.
[3] UN document A/S-12/PV.21, 23 June 1982, p. 91.

4   UN document A/S-12/PV.23, 25 June 1982, p. 16.
5   UN document A/S-12/PV.17, 21 June 1982, p. 38.
6   UN document A/S-12/PV.22, 22 June 1982, p. 17.
7   UN document A/S-12/PV.18, 22 June 1982, p. 26.
8   UN document A/S-12/PV.8, 12 June 1982, pp. 39 and 42.
9   UN document A/S-12/PV.14, 19 June 1982, pp. 13 and 16.
10 UN document A/S-12/PV.14, 19 June 1982, pp. 23 and 24.
11 UN document A/S-12/PV.17, 21 June 1982, pp. 126 and 127.
12 UN document A/S-12/PV.17, 21 June 1982, p. 74.
13 UN document A/S-12/PV.7, 12 June 1982, p. 32.
14 UN document A/S-12/PV.9, 15 June 1982, p. 59.
15 UN document A/S-12/PV.6, 12 June 1982, pp. 26 and 27.
16 UN document A/S-12/PV.10, 16 June 1982, p. 51.
17 UN document A/S-12/PV.24, 26 June 1982, p. 36.
18 UN document A/S-12/PV.25, 23 June 1982, p. 61.
19 UN document A/S-12/PV.9, 15 June 1982, pp. 28 and 31.
20 UN document A/S-12/PV.8, 12 June 1982, p. 12.
21 UN document A/S-12/PV.18, 22 June 1982, p. 7.
22 UN document A/S-12/PV.17, 21 June 1982, pp. 62 and 63.
23 UN document A/S-12/PV.19, 22 June 1982, p. 26.
24 UN document A/S-12/PV.25, 26 June 1982, p. 28.
25 UN document A/S-12/PV.11, 17 June 1982, p. 11.
26 UN document A/S-12/PV.4, 9 June 1982, p. 11.
27 UN document A/S-12/PV.14, 19 June 1982, pp. 45 and 46.
28 UN document A/S-12/PV.15, 21 June 1982, p. 19.
29 UN document A/S-12/PV.13, 19 June 1982, pp. 42 and 43.
30 UN document A/S-12/PV.15, 21 June 1982, p. 46.
31 UN document A/S-12/PV.6, 12 June 1982, p. 41.
32 UN document A/S-12/PV.8, 12 June 1982, p. 27.
33 UN document A/S-12/PV.22, 22 June 1982, p. 37.
34 UN document A/S-12/PV.5, 11 June 1982, p. 7.
35 UN document A/S-12/PV.15, 21 June 1982, p. 63.
36 UN document A/S-12/PV.2, 9 June 1982, p. 67.
37 UN document A/S-12/PV.21, 23 June 1982, p. 61.
38 UN document A/S-12/PV.22, 22 June 1982, pp. 52 and 53.
39 UN document A/S-12/PV.20, 23 June 1982, p. 16.
40 UN document A/S-12/PV.12, 18 June 1982, pp. 22 and 23.
41 UN document A/S-12/PV.24, 26 June 1982, p. 4.
42 UN document A/S-12/PV.13, 19 June 1982, p. 97.

Appendix IV.   UN Resolutions adopted in 1983

Convention on the prohibition of nuclear weapons
(UN General Assembly Resolution 38/73, 15 December 1983)

The General Assembly,

Alarmed by the threat to the survival of mankind and to the life-sustaining system posed by nuclear weapons and by their use, inherent in concepts of deterrence,

Conscious of an increased danger of nuclear war as a result of the intensification of the nuclear arms race and the serious deterioration of the international situation,

Convinced that nuclear disarmament is essential for the prevention of nuclear war and for the strengthening of international peace and security,

Further convinced that a prohibition of the use or threat of use of nuclear weapons would be a step towards the complete elimination of nuclear weapons leading to general and complete disarmament under strict and effective international control,

Recalling its declaration, contained in the Final Document of the Tenth Special Session of the General Assembly, that all States should actively participate in efforts to bring about conditions in international relations among States in which a code of peaceful conduct of nations in international affairs could be agreed upon which would preclude the use or threat of use of nuclear weapons,[18]

Reaffirming the declaration that the use of nuclear weapons would be a violation of the Charter of the United Nations and a crime against humanity, contained in its resolutions 1653 (XVI) of 24 November 1961, 33/71 B of 14 December 1978, 34/83 G of 11 December 1979, 35/152 D of 12 December 1980 and 36/92 I of 9 December 1981,

Noting with regret that the Committee on Disarmament, during its session in 1983, was not able to undertake negotiations with a view to achieving agreement on an international convention prohibiting the use or threat of use of nuclear weapons under any circumstances, taking as a basis the text contained in General Assembly resolution 37/100 C of 13 December 1982,

1. *Reiterates its request* to the Committee on Disarmament[19] to commence negotiations, as a matter of priority, in order to achieve agreement on an international convention prohibiting the use or threat of use of nuclear weapons under any cir-

---

[18]   Resolution S-10/2, para. 58.
[19]   From the date of commencement of the annual session in 1984, the Committee on Disarmament will be known as the "Conference on Disarmament" (see *Official Records of the General Assembly, Thirty-eighth Session, Supplement No. 27* (A/38/27, para. 21).

cumstances, taking as a basis the annexed draft Convention on the Prohibition of the Use of Nuclear Weapons;

2. *Further requests* the Committee on Disarmament to report on the results of those negotiations to the General Assembly at its thirty-ninth session.

Condemnation of nuclear war
(UN General Assembly Resolution 38/75, 15 December 1983)

The General Assembly,

Expressing its alarm at the growing threat of nuclear war, which can lead to the destruction of civilization on earth,

Drawing the attention of all States and peoples to the conclusions arrived at by the most eminent scientists and military and civilian experts to the effect that it is impossible to limit the deadly consequences of nuclear war if it is ever begun and that in a nuclear war there can be no victors,

Convinced that the prevention of nuclear catastrophe is the most profound aspiration of billions of people on earth,

Reaffirming its call for the conclusion of an international convention on the prohibition of the use of nuclear weapons with the participation of all the nuclear-weapon States,

1. *Resolutely, unconditionally and for all time condemns* nuclear war as being contrary to human conscience and reason, as the most monstrous crime against peoples and as a violation of the foremost human right—the right to life;

2. *Condemns* the formulation, propounding, dissemination and propaganda of political and military doctrines and concepts intended to provide "legitimacy" for the first use of nuclear weapons and in general to justify the "admissibility" of unleashing nuclear war;

3. *Calls upon* all States to unite and redouble their efforts aimed at removing the threat of nuclear war, halting the nuclear arms race and reducing nuclear weapons until they are completely eliminated.

Index

First use *and* No-first-use *refer to nuclear weapons*